MW00619254

I'm a Memphian.

Character references for a city filled with it and often absolutely full of it.

By Dan Conaway

The Nautilus Publishing Company

Cover design by Chung Design
Illustrations by Connor Covert
Art Direction by Maggie White

For bulk orders and educational discounts, contact:

The Nautilus Publishing Company
426 S. Lamar Blvd., Suite 16
Oxford, MS 38655
Tel: 662-513-0159
info@nautiluspublishing.com

Conaway, Dan (1949-)
I'm a Memphian — 1st ed.
ISBN: 978-1-936946-21-1

PRINTED IN CANADA
through a partnership with Friesens Printing

10 9 8 7 6 5 4 3 2 1

The painting on the cover, "Historic Encounter Between E.H. Crump and W.C. Handy on Beale St." (1964) is by iconic Memphis artist, Carroll Cloar, and is used by permission of the artist's family.

The quintessential Memphis characters depicted in the piece are (from left) Charles Diehl, Watkins Overton, W.C. Handy, "Shifty" Logan, E.H. Crump, Clarence Saunders, Lt. George W. Lee, Senator Kenneth McKellar, and Arthur Halle, with Press-Scimitar reporter Clark Porteus in the background, and paperboy and downtown fixture Tony "Monk" Cassatta to the side.

To Nora, Hallie and Gaines – my Memphians.

"...the most ordinary of origins
have sent such extraordinary
gifts to the world from here."

All Funked Up

Memphasis, my new weekly column in *The Daily News*, begins Friday, April 9, and will appear every Friday and over the weekend in *The Memphis News*, the paper's weekly. It's all about what I think Memphis is all about. Let me know what you think. But think first. There's far too little of that going around.

As published April 9, 2010

Face it. You're funky. ***funky 1* |*f ng k*|** *adjective (funkier, funkiest) informal 1 (of music) having or using a strong dance rhythm, in particular that of funk: some excellent funky beats. • modern and stylish in an unconventional or striking way : she likes wearing funky clothes. 2 strongly musty: cooked greens make the kitchen smell really funky.*

Rufus Thomas understood. If a chicken could get funky, it would be in Memphis. Just look at the definition. It includes quintessential Memphis words. Rhythm. Beats. Unconventional. Striking. And, yes, greens and kitchen are in there, too.

This part of the world, and Memphis as its capital, gave the rest of the world rhythm and blues, the beat of rock and roll, the king and court of unconventional and striking. And, yes, we gave them greens and cornbread, too, and grits and chitterlings and fried green tomatoes and fried chicken.

We gave them the stuff that sustains life in hard-to-live lives. Soul-stirring music born of abject poverty. Mouthwatering flavor from food easy to come by out in the yard, over in the field. A sense of, "I can make it," "I can change it," "I can create it," because the most ordinary of origins have sent such extra extraordinary gifts to the world from here.

Elvis and Holiday Inns. Self-service groceries and Federal Express. Three 6 Mafia and modern orthopedics. Stax and St. Jude. Isaac, Al and B.B. Clarence, Fred and Kemmons. Billy Dunavant and Billy Kyle. Pit barbecue and Pitt Hyde.

We have over the years in no particular order and without argument been known as the world's foremost city for cotton, hardwood, juke joints, mules, blues, rock 'n roll, yellow fever, soul, keelboater fights, air freight, trauma nails, and barbecue.

And the assassination of Martin Luther King, Jr.

All of that, mixed in our rich and dangerously spicy diversity, baked in our sweat-through-everything summers, and left to stand on the kitchen, restaurant and church tables where we all gather, has made us one of the funkiest dishes this country serves. And people from everywhere can't wait for a taste.

We're known the world over for the beat of our mojo, for the depth and breadth of our creativity, the warmth of our hospitality, and as the most giving city of our size anywhere. Yet, if you listen to us, you'd never know it.

We think it's all about crime – or who the mayor is, was, or isn't – or consolidation – or taxes – or what we'll do about my street/neighborhood/school/Bible/gun. Those are real concerns needing real solutions, but people from everywhere have them, and when we bitch mightily as if they were ours uniquely, we can lose sight of what others see in us.

Look at it this way, if everybody sees that funky person you're with as attractive, fun, imaginative, intelligent, capable, different, open and loaded with potential and you don't…you're the one who's wrong. As John Cleese purportedly said, "If you walk into a room dressed in a suit and everyone else is dressed as a chicken, you're the one who's out of place." Rufus would have understood.

Work on our faults, but build on our strengths.

I'm a Memphian, and I'm funky.

"Barbecue in Memphis
is quite simply the highest
a pig can go."

Pig Ultimate

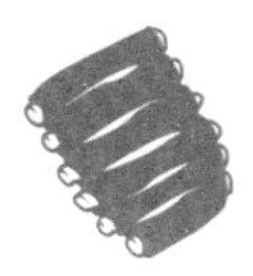

Thanks for all the responses to the *Memphasis* debut on April 9. Many of you sent me encouraging notes and passed it along to friends. A few of you provided grammatical instruction or fact checks. Or both. Well, here I am again. And, yes, I know that the preceding "or both" is a sentence fragment.

This week we're having barbecue.

As published April 16, 2010

If you don't get your barbecue in Memphis, it doesn't matter where you get it.

Any pig cooked for a considerable amount of time with any care is going to taste pretty good, but, in this town, that doesn't make it barbecue. We have elevated that term to legendary status. We are to barbecue what Kleenex is to facial tissue, what Coke is to all soft drinks in the South. We are barbecue.

A pizza chain has defiled it by producing something called Memphis Barbecue Pizza, covered in chicken. Clucking chicken. The McRib … a fast-food, fake-rib, pickle-covered, sweet-sauce-slathered sandwich … might be fine elsewhere. Serving it here should be a felony. As you wander the world and see a sign somewhere that says Memphis Barbecue, run. It won't make you homesick, just sick. It will be to barbecue what karaoke is to The Rolling Stones, and you won't get no satisfaction. Barbecue in Memphis is quite simply the highest a pig can go. A pig, people. Not any other creature, not even processed pork, but a whole or a recognizable part of a pig.

Our reputation is at stake, so let's review.

If it doesn't involve a dead pig, it's not barbecue. A beef rib, while a challenging thing and not without flavor or merit as a fungo bat or a handy club, is not barbecue. Brisket and barbecue both begin with a b. There ends the similarity. Chicken can be prepared a thousand satisfying ways. None of them is barbecue. Goat, cooked oh-so-slow and basted in an oh-so perfect and time-honored blend of seasonings, is, well, a goat. It's not barbecue.

If it does involve liquid smoke, it's not barbecue. I've driven through liquid smoke, gotten some in my eye in a bar, even felt it immediately following that shrimp dish with the four red peppers next to it on the menu. I don't want any of that on my pork shoulder.

If the sauce is from foreign shores … say Kansas City, Texas or North Carolina … it's not barbecue. France sent us Hollandaise sauce. Tasty. Not barbecue. And even using the right sauce or seasoning doesn't make something barbecue any more than dressing up like Elvis makes you able to sing a lick. Cherry cough drops aren't cherries. Potato chips aren't barbecue.

Barbecue is not a verb. You don't barbecue anything. If you're fortunate enough to be given the skill, and you have a whole pig or some portion thereof, you can cook, or smoke, or make, or fix a whole mess of barbecue. You don't eat a process.

Barbecue is not a place or a device. I'm not going to a barbecue, just like I'm not going to the corner of steak and onion rings. If there's anything red hot on my patio, I'm not calling it a barbecue, and I'm not putting anything on a barbecue except slaw and sauce. You don't eat an event. Or a grill. Or a cooker. Or a pit.

These are the essentials. Spelling doesn't matter. Barbecue. Bar-b-que. Bar-B-Q. Q. BBQ. For ribs, wet or dry can be legitimately debated. For shoulder, pulled or chopped are both acceptable. Long enough is the right cooking time … you can take a weekend to cook a whole hog and The Rendezvous cooks their ribs in about an hour. It's the intrinsic nature, the soul if you will, of Memphis barbecue that has eliminated the need to modify it with Memphis. Real Hollandaise is French, and the stuff on chain restaurant Benedicts is not. Real barbecue is Memphis, and anything else is not.

I'm a Memphian, and so is barbecue.

"Americans stand out in
Europe like Hawaiian shirts
at a funeral."

Worldview

We seem to worry a lot about who we aren't, what we aren't and where we aren't. Memphians are always asking, "What in the world will they make of that?" Well, in my experience, we seem to make the world happy. Not a bad thing.

This week begins in Paris.

As published April 23, 2010

You may not know them, but they know you.

Paris.

Cabs in Paris are about the size of clown cars, and putting more than three passengers in one has the same effect. So, when the five of us arrived – us, our kids and my mother-in-law – we split up in two cabs. Gaines, five at the time, and I had the all-guy cab. The front seat passenger was a dog, part poodle and part Charles De Gaulle, complete with his water bowl in the passenger well. The driver introduced him as, "le navigateur." The driver spoke no English. I spoke even less French. Somehow, with Gaines and the dog laughing at both of us, I realized he was asking me where we were from – a place, not a country. He knew we were Americans. Americans stand out in Europe like Hawaiian shirts at a funeral. "Memphis," I said. What happened next was a six-ticket ride. He took a hard right, and a death-defying run around the Arc de Triomphe on the Champs-Elysées. A couple hundred lanes of traffic anarchy. Like NASCAR, except no caution flags and less courtesy. Sweeping into a side street and braking hard enough to turn over Charles De Gaulle's water bowl and my stomach, he stopped in front of a nightclub. Sticking out of the wall was the rear end of a 1959 pink Caddy. "Elvis!" the driver exclaimed.

Amsterdam.

So we're in line with another Memphis couple at the Anne Frank House. It's going to be a while, so the guys go to get everybody a snack. French fries. Stands sell them everywhere in Amsterdam. With mayonnaise. No, really. But I digress. One particular stand gets our business because the entire thing was painted with the scene from the Sistine Chapel where Michelangelo depicts God giving life to Adam … except, in this case, God is giving Adam an order of French fries. "French fries," I said. "What part of the southern United States are you from?" the vendor asked in perfect English. "Memphis," I drawled. "Friendliest city I know," he said. Seems he takes his family to the United States for two weeks every year, picking a different state for the whole two weeks. Been to Memphis twice. "We had the children with us one night, having a wonderful time walking around when we got a little lost," he related. "We walked several dark blocks when we saw spinning bright lights. Black people, white people dancing and laughing," he said, laughing himself. "They adopted us, gave us huge beers, taught the kids new dances … and called us a cab. Best time we had on that whole trip. Can't remember the name … it's, uh …," he struggled. "Raiford's Hollywood?" I guessed. "Yes, yes," he said, clapping his hands together, "that's it!"

You can't make this stuff up.

I have three packages of Memphis cigarettes from Germany, and a Memphis ashtray I talked a bar owner out of in Munich. I walked by a Volkswagen Memphis model in Salzburg, and I've been to a show in Rome featuring work from a whole design school called Memphis.

In Galatoire's in New Orleans … yes, that's an international city … the waiter engages us in conversation with a heavier European accent than the French fry guy in Holland. "Where are you from?" We tell him. He doesn't tell us about the signature trout or crab dishes, or the wine list, or anything about one of the country's great menus. He simply asks, "So where do you go for your barbecue?"

I'm a Memphian, and I'm world famous.

"If we were all the same,
what a great large snore
life would be."

Howard and Bill

Just as this city is different from any other, each of us is different. If we were all the same, what a great large snore life would be. However, if we fail to respect our differences, or fail to treat each other with simple dignity and common courtesy, what a nightmare awaits us all.

This week you'll meet Howard and Bill.

As published April 30, 2010

Two halves make a whole.

In the 60s, Howard Robertson was a black postal carrier moonlighting as a waiter at the capital of white money dining in Memphis, Justine's, housed in an antebellum mansion. Bill Loeb was a successful white businessman, owner of ubiquitous laundry branches about town, and the brother of Henry Loeb, mayor during the 1968 sanitation strike. Loeb lived in a home literally bordering the Memphis Country Club. Robertson lived in the other Memphis those of us who grew up white then never really acknowledged.

They would meet amid crisp white tablecloths set with crystal and crabmeat, one hosting, the other serving.

One evening at Justine's, Robertson did something that displeased Loeb. In front of his guests and the entire restaurant, Loeb wore him out. Loud and personal. Putting someone "in his place." But that wasn't Robertson's place. He returned the verbal fire, shot for shot, then returned to the kitchen and quit. That took the kind of dignity and courage that comes from deep inside. The kind that says even though this will cause sacrifice for my family, even though that kind of behavior was the norm, I will not take it. Loeb's brother, Henry, would later see that sentiment expressed on posters, "I am a man."

This is when this becomes a different story. This is when Loeb would show his own dignity and courage. As he talked with his guests, he realized he had been in the wrong. He invited all of them back the following evening, and asked for Robertson. When told he had quit, Loeb asked Justine if she could please try and get him there. It took some doing, but she did, and for the second night in a row, Loeb and Robertson became the center of attention for the restaurant. Except, this night, Loeb apologized. Man to man. They talked. They decided to meet again.

And they kept meeting for the rest of Loeb's life. They watched games together. They talked life. They talked business. When Loeb converted his laundries to very popular barbecue shops, he brought Robertson on as a partner in two of them.

That was then, and that is now. The sense of two cities in one, a tale like Dickens' "It was the best of times, it was the worst of times," is not only still with us, it divides and defeats us. What Robertson and Loeb did, when it was much more difficult to do, is the common ground we must all find.

Bill Loeb's children have continued to show leadership in the business, arts and causes of our city. Howard Robertson's son – Howard, Jr. – is an involved citizen and business owner, and married to the executive director of the National Civil Rights Museum. Howard, Jr. once told me, "A father is how a son learns to be a man."

Good job, guys, you taught them well, and there's a lesson in it for us.

I'm a Memphian, hopefully, like Howard and Bill.

"You walk by a dumpster and step over a couple of puddles of God-knows-what to get in."

One Of A Kind

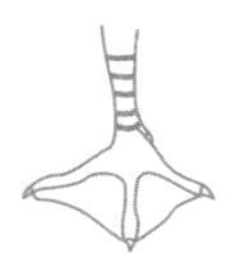

A number of places have a certain thing about them that is aptly described as unique, but just one or two things in most cases. Duck Hill, Mississippi, for instance, has trees that grow damn near sideways out of that namesake hill. It takes a bunch of things like that before the whole place can be thought of as unique.

Folks, this place is unique.

As published June 11, 2010

Really unique is really not. Memphis is.

Nothing is really unique. Unique is unique. If there is more than one of it, it isn't.

Memphis is et up with unique.

The Peabody is unique. Two hammered duck hunters dump their live decoys in the lobby fountain. One is actually the hotel manager, and instead of getting him fired, that drunken prank makes the place world-famous. Almost 80 years later, ducks are still in that fountain by day, live in an air-conditioned penthouse by night, march back and forth twice a day to a packed crowd, and are on TV as much as Daffy and Donald.

Unique.

Graceland is unique. Depending on who you talk to, Elvis has been dead since 1977. Visit Graceland today and tell me you don't think he's still in there somewhere. Somebody has just been napping on that ginormous couch. Those dark TVs are still warm, and somebody's screwing around with a guitar in the jungle room. Walk by the kitchen and you can smell peanut butter and banana sandwiches. There's a reason they won't let us go upstairs.

Unique.

Memphis in May is unique. "I've got an idea," someone certifiable said at the first meeting, "Let's have a barbecue cooking contest. Contestants will come from all over the world, bring smokers that look like locomotives, set up booths 30 feet tall, and 100,000-plus will come down to the river to watch them cook food they can't eat."

Unique.

The National Civil Rights Museum is unique. There is one Lorraine Motel, one balcony, one bathroom window through which a modern-day prophet was killed but his dream refused to die. What fed that dream and what feeds it still is on display in one place.

Unique.

St. Jude Children's Research Hospital is unique. What all those unbelievably dedicated people drink over there isn't Kool-Aid, it's great big gulps of hope. What they do every day to give children a chance at life shines a bright light from Memphis the whole world can see.

Unique.

The Rendezvous is unique. It's in a basement. You walk by a dumpster and step over a couple of puddles of God-knows-what to get in. Not only do they charbroil their ribs down there, the restaurant itself has burned twice. The beams are still charred. Everything in this city's collective attic is hanging on the walls or from the ceiling. Their ribs started and continue to fuel a worldwide debate. Wet or dry.

Unique.

Cozy Corner is unique, a barbecue joint famous for … Cornish hens? The National Ornamental Metal Museum is unique, both for what it is and the river view from where it is. Dyer's is unique, deep frying hamburgers in a vat of grease I think Andy Jackson brought with him when he founded the city.

The list goes on and on, and that's the point. Beyond and because of music, and barbecue, and cotton, and race, and hospitality, and river, and creativity, it goes all the way to soul. Uniquely.

I'm a Memphian, and I'm unique.

"The truth of what you see every day in Memphis is better than the fiction other cities have to come up with to make them interesting."

Look Who's Here

If you let it, the passing parade that is this city will pass you by. If you pause to take it in, a chimp might sell you a suit.

As published June 25, 2010

"38 regular," I told the chimp.

Take a minute and look around. You may see a story. And it may last a lifetime.

Before he was Prince Mongo, he was Robert Hodges. Oh, he was clearly from a place far, far away, but he had not yet assumed the title. When I first became aware of him, the heir apparent to the house of hinky used to ride around town on a motorcycle in a leather jacket and goggles. Sitting behind him was a chimp … in matching leather jacket and goggles. It was the late 60s, and sightings of the weird and wonderful, both natural and chemically-induced, were commonplace, but this caught your attention.

Hodges owned a men's store in those days … no, really … called Dalian et Rae. I went in there one day to look around and saw no one, no one human at least. The chimp appeared from behind a clothes rack, in a nice little jacket and pants, and held up his hand. At this point, you have to make a decision – either go for the whole experience or turn around and walk out. Either way, you've got a story, but what makes Memphis Memphis is that the stories can always get better.

I took his hand.

He walked me to the men's suits, and stepped back as if to say, "You look like a 38 regular." That's where he stopped, and that … a couple thousand super-sized fries ago … was my size. He smiled, and, buddy, chimps can smile. I was about to ask him, I swear, what he had in a double-breasted blazer, when I heard a voice. No, not the chimp, but a guy who worked there who had been in the storeroom. I never saw the chimp again but his bananas owner went on to cosmic infamy.

The truth of what you can see every day in Memphis is better than the fiction other cities have to come up with to make them interesting.

Like that day in 1965 when a 16-year-old in his momma's convertible pulled up to the light at Union and Cooper. A Harley pulled up next to him, and, with a big smile, Elvis said to the kid, "Nice car." I might still be sitting at that light if the guy behind me hadn't laid on the horn.

Or the time I ran into Isaac Hayes in a break room and we spent an hour talking about bathroom renovation and fireplaces.

Or when I was screwing around with a wedge in my parents' front yard when Cary Middlecoff walked by, and spent 30 minutes showing me how to hit down on the ball.

I have hundreds more, and whether you realize it or not, so do you. Start looking around for your stories. They're everywhere in this town because giants … giant heroes, giant goats, giant characters … have walked and continue to walk among us.

I'm a Memphian, and I have a story.

“His is a quintessential
Memphis story, a roller
coaster ride from rock
bottom to dizzying
height and back again.”

Keedoozle Of A Story

"Piggly Wiggly...ain't that a funny name? The fellow who got that name up must have a screw loose somewheres."

So said the fellow who got that name up in 1916 and used it to introduce the world to self-service shopping from right here in Memphis.

And when it came to big ideas with funny names, he was just getting started.

As published November 12, 2010

Clarence Saunders was all that and a bag of groceries.

The difference between Fitzgerald's Great Gatsby and our own Clarence Saunders is that Gatsby is fiction. Both were fabulously wealthy, self-made, flamboyant masters of the 1920s. One is a famous literary work. The other is a famous piece of work who changed the way everyone lives.

Clarence Saunders invented – and patented – self-service grocery stores in 1916 with the first Piggly Wiggly at Jefferson and Main.

That's a fact. But facts don't make stories; they are simply ingredients that inform the process. The flavor comes from how skillfully the dish is made. The smell of it is also based on that skill.

Clarence Saunders was a spice rack.

Fact is – he built the Pink Palace from Italian marble, put in a golf course, and never lived a single day or shanked a single wedge there. Ah, but the story.

Story I heard from old men around tables was he bought that property and built the most ostentatious house possible and his own golf course on it because it was across the street from the Memphis Country Club. They wouldn't let this upstart who dropped out of school at 14, stumbled into town at 21, and stunned the world at 35 into their club or on their golf course. So he built one they couldn't play on and a house they couldn't miss when they played theirs. Today the house is a museum and that golf course is Chickasaw Gardens.

Fact is – he lost all of that in a failed attempt to corner the stock market in 1923.

Story I got across reputable bars was that he took on the New York Stock Exchange after they tried a bear raid to devalue the Piggly Wiggly stock. By their own rules, he won, but they changed the rules after the fact and Saunders was ruined. He wasn't a member of that club either.

Fact is – unable to use the Piggly Wiggly name; he started another chain with the snappy moniker of *Clarence Saunders Sole Owner Of My Name Stores*, recovered his fortune, and lost it again in the Great Depression. He even started a football team, kicking off another story.

Notable bookies say after Saunders' Tigers beat the Green Bay Packers in 1929, a guy from the Decatur Staleys asked the team to join a league his buddies were starting. Saunders said no because he didn't like to travel. The league was the National Football League, the guy was George Halas, and the Staleys became the Chicago Bears.

Oh well.

Before he died in 1953, he started two automated store concepts – *Keedoozle and Foodelectric* – forerunners of self-checkout that only failed because his vision was ahead of the technology to realize it.

His is a quintessential Memphis story, a roller coaster ride from rock bottom to dizzying height and back again, real genius mixed with hardheaded inflexibility and super-sized personality, widely known around the world except, of course, for here.

I'm a Memphian, and that's a fact and a story.

“I went to an all-but-unknown
park dedicated to an
all-but-forgotten war and
found my brother.”

Connecting

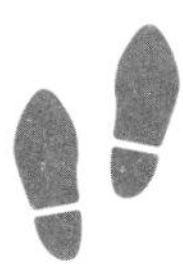

Memphis is full of interesting nooks and crannies worth exploration. Some we've seen so many times we don't see them at all anymore. Some are so tucked away by time and neglect that they're hidden from view and interest. Some you think you've seen, but there may be much more beyond your expectation.

You may find a bit of you.

As published December 3, 2010

Around here, if you look closely, you'll find a connection.

"The Hiker" is a statue guarding the corner of East Parkway and Central from any further attacks from Spain. In 1898, dressed just like this in a great hat, sleeves rolled up just so, holding a rifle just like that, he remembered the Maine and charged up Cuba's San Juan Hill.

And, evidently, there are zero degrees of separation between him, the Spanish-American War, William Randolph Hearst, Teddy Roosevelt, a float down the Mississippi to New Orleans (almost), fraternity row at LSU, the jail in Baton Rouge, my brother ... and me.

You see, I was going to write this column about the only park in Memphis dedicated to veterans of a foreign war. No, not the two big ones. Not Korea or Vietnam. Not the first Gulf War or either of the current two.

The Spanish-American War has its own park, a gently sloping 1.8 acres of green with "The Hiker" right in the middle of it. It was built in a former railroad right-of-way in 1956 and while many of us drive by it every day, few know what it is.

I knew that Hearst needed a war to build readership for his newspaper empire and when the USS Maine sunk in the Havana harbor, he got his shot and his slogan "Remember the Maine!"

I knew that Teddy Roosevelt needed to heroically charge up something somewhere to build his political résumé, and Cuba gave him his hill.

What I didn't know until I read the plaque on the statue's base was the name of the veterans' commander who led the effort to establish the park. When I read that name, I was suddenly ten years old, standing on the cobblestones, and seeing my big brother, Frank, off on an epic summer adventure to float the river to the Big Easy.

The name on the plaque is Fred Bauer, and he was the grandfather of the Fred Bauer who was Frank's companion on that journey. The conveyance was a houseboat, dragged from beneath the river and restored, sort of. Other than a very old, not very big outboard for emergencies only – like surviving barge wake tsunamis – the only power source was the current and the only steering came from poles.

Spun like a top for hundreds of miles, bailing constantly to stay afloat, they got all the way to Baton Rouge and got a little drunk – okay, a lot drunk – and decided, since they were Kappa Sigs in college, the LSU chapter would put them up for the night.

When the housemother saw two bearded, bedraggled, and thoroughly hammered river rats "stealing" a loaf of bread from the kitchen, she screamed – and it turns out the Baton Rouge jail would put them up for the night.

Come morning, charges were dropped, the trip and houseboat abandoned, and the story assured.

I went to an all-but-unknown park dedicated to an all-but-forgotten war and found my brother.

I'm a Memphian, and I'll bet we're connected.

“Old sanctuaries became new gyms and those gyms became new sanctuaries.”

An Uncommon Man In Common

Most of us have been fortunate enough to have a number of people who positively shaped our lives growing up, who saw in us a special something and helped us see it in ourselves. Parents, as in plural. Family. Teachers. Coaches. Ministers. Friends.

Too many of us have had too few people like that in their lives. Too many obstacles. Too many boundaries. Too little hope.

But they did have one.

As published February 4, 2011

An uncommon man in common.

The first one was in the former Barksdale police station, a mounted police station complete with a stable and cells. Kids playing horse replaced the horses. Cells became offices, and the squad room turned into a classroom. A pool table took the place of the sergeant's desk, kids doing homework replaced cops doing paperwork, and those with nowhere to go and nothing better to do found both and themselves in the first Boys Club.

Others would follow. In abandoned churches and schools. In old YMCAs. In the projects. On troubled corners and challenged streets. Old sanctuaries became new gyms and those gyms became new sanctuaries. New purpose was found, new life discovered for structures and people. These places aren't made from just bricks and mortar, from wood and steel. They are made from sterner stuff.

They are made from Bernal Smith.

Lawyers and doctors, social workers and scientists, corporate shooting stars and NBA shooting guards, teachers and preachers, linemen and fashion line designers, successful men and women with the humblest of Memphis childhoods, the least of prospects, the dimmest of hopes have returned over the years from all over the world to share their stories with club kids.

They came because Bernal Smith asked them, and because he was in every one of those stories.

For 43 years, he was the father where there wasn't one, the positive role model where there wasn't one, the alternative to the streets, the corners and the alleys when there was no one at home, or the wrong ones at home.

I met him when we were both young men. He looked at me, and said, like he had said and would say to thousands, "Come over here and let me show you how we do this." Then he taught me how to make hobo stew. Over the next four decades he would teach me about selflessness and commitment. He would show me how to see the promise in a kid's eyes the first time he saw a sky full of stars over a lake, the first time she saw her name on an award. He would do that not by lecturing or drawing attention to himself but, just like that hobo stew, by example.

When Bernal Smith was there, it was never about him. And he was always there.

Now there are six Boys & Girls Clubs here, plus a Technical Training Center and Camp Phoenix, serving something like 7,000 young people. In Bernal's eyes, the measure of the clubs' success would never be size and scope, but rather the progress of each of those children, their lives the proof of our worth to society.

By that lasting and meaningful measure, he might just be the most successful person I've ever had the pleasure to know.

My friend died last week and they tell me they're going to name one of the clubs after him. That won't be his honor. That will be ours.

I'm a Memphian, and I knew Bernal Smith.

“Three slices of very white bread were in somebody else’s kitchen.”

Paradise Found

Got my mojo working, but it just won't work on you
Got my mojo working, but it just won't work on you
I wanna love you so bad till I don't know what to do

Muddy Waters, Club Paradise, 1964

As published March 18, 2011

A bright blue night.

Just about any weekend anybody in the Gant button-down crowd could catch a concert at the Coliseum or Ellis Auditorium, crash a party at Clearpool, or hear a great band in a gym somewhere in Weejun town. This was Memphis in the early '60s. You could see Elvis at a stoplight, Jerry Lee in a restaurant, and listen to Wooly Bully on the radio waiting in line for auto inspection right in front of Sam the Sham's club.

But this weekend was different. This was Club Paradise. Howling Wolf and Muddy Waters were sharing the stage. The little red rooster was going to take on the hoochie coochie man. Ba-bah-ba-bump. One would moan at midnight while the other got his mojo working. Ba-bah-ba-bump.

And we were going.

Way down there, down where we'd never been, in the middle of where we weren't supposed to go. We weren't, however, telling our parents. There was a limit to our courage.

We were big, bad and ready. Nobody was going to mess with us.

Duke was the oldest, pushing 16, five eleven and all of a buck sixty five. I was two weeks past 15, about five nine and a buck fifty. His little brother, Chris, finished out the threesome at barely 14, five and not much, and the Zippo in my pocket weighed more than he did. Their parents were going out, so we stole their mother's car. Duke drove, with no license, I handled the city map under the dome light, with no clue, and Chris was in charge of the radio. After a few wide-eyed wrong turns, we slid that east Memphis station wagon into the Club Paradise parking lot on Georgia Avenue, eased through the door, and paid our cover.

Three slices of very white bread were in somebody else's kitchen.

"Oh the dogs begin to bark, and the hound begin to howl," Howling Wolf growled from somewhere up front, and a table full of folks asked us to join them. Somebody handed me a big brown bottle, a big woman gave little Chris a hug, and all of us started laughing. "Oh watch out strange kind people, cause little red rooster is on the prowl," Howling Wolf sang, and the rest of the night was a song.

Way down there, down where we'd never been, in the middle of where we weren't supposed to go everything was different. And the same. Our lives were in different worlds, our futures sharing common ground. Completely independent of each other, and utterly dependent.

Sometimes it seems we lived then and live now in parallel dimensions. There is real magic when nights like that occur, when we are bound by laughter, by music, by what we share rather than by what we fear.

We got home, got the car back in the garage as if nothing had changed. But, for at least one night, everything had and it seemed everything could.

I'm a Memphian, and I've been to Club Paradise.

"You're looking at a place
where things come from
everywhere and go
everywhere else."

Two Ways To Look At It

Most cities are looking for something to hang a civic hat on – a single thing that can define and attract and separate.

Might be they're the birthplace of something or someone significant enough to brand a whole city. Or perhaps they're known as the center or capital of some enterprise, the place where something is made or from or named after.

If they're really lucky, really rare as cities go, they'll have more than one such thing and a few, incredibly few, might have such things from both the right and left brain, both cool and profitable.

Of course, they'd have to realize it.

As published April 8, 2011

It all depends on your point of view.

Coming from Arkansas, it looks like Oz.

It appears suddenly, just past that truck in front of you, between that truck and the one next to you, glimpsed between rearview mirror checks of that truck behind you. You've somehow survived the concrete gauntlet of West Memphis and the semi cowboys whipping their rigs into a frenzy, driving them to market across the modern day trails of I-40 and I-55.

There in front of you is a city on a hill. It's an urban island; surrounded by the agrarian sea of cotton, soybeans and rice you've just navigated. You'll reach it by crossing a bridge of lights and a river so great that a great nation uses it to define its east and west. You see the city spread out across the horizon, and to my taste, a feast for both eyes and spirit.

Okay, that's a truckload of metaphors, but I think the view is pretty trucking impressive.

You're looking at a place where new ideas come out of nowhere and go everywhere, where cultures, races, circumstances and history all come together and give rise to new ways to see, hear and heal. From here – from a brand-new waterfront town and a 30-story stainless steel pyramid on one side to an old city makeover and fledgling arts district on the other – you can't see the problems, but you can still see the possibilities.

Coming from Mississippi, it looks like a Star Wars set.

It appears to the right, just past that truck in front of you, between that truck and the one next to you, glimpsed between rearview mirror checks of that truck behind you. You've somehow survived the challenge of the Lamar corridor where Mississippi turns into Tennessee and farm turns into industry as suddenly and chaotically as a five-truck pileup.

There beside you at Shelby Drive is the old Tennessee Yard, the new Memphis Intermodal Facility. BNSF dropped a $200 million upgrade here and rolled in those ginormous cranes that look like Empire war engines and can lift the national debt. The wheels are bigger than my house. They pick up 40-foot containers from railcars and put them on trucks and vice versa, and they do that 600,000 times a year with capacity to do it a million times a year.

You're looking at a place where things come from everywhere

and go everywhere else, where river, rail, air, road and geography all come together. From here – from the permanent ruts in the road made by the world's heavy loads – you can see what made Memphis storage closet and delivery service to the known universe.

Two views, one of a city of imagination, an incubator where new things are born and grow strong in the Delta heat, and another of a city of purpose, a critical transfer point where whatever's wanted comes to be sorted and sent.

One city.

I'm a Memphian, and our original music includes the sounds of boats, trains, trucks and planes.

"Figuratively or literally ...
you will return to where
it all began."

A Shared Journey

Everybody's from somewhere, and, if you grew up there or family before you did, that somewhere has something to do with the someone you become. Figuratively or literally, perhaps to measure progress or check direction, to find affirmation or peace, you will return to where it all began.

Godspeed.

As published April 15, 2011

True North.

My oldest big brother fell recently. He took a header off the basement steps and landed on his hip. He lives in the Adirondacks, 15 miles from any group of anything larger than four, if you don't count critters. His wife can't pick him up, and their two labs, well trained as they are, can't fetch an orthopedist.

We were supposed to go fishing in May with my other big brother.

We're years, careers, and more than a thousand miles apart, my brothers and I. Our kids are spread from New York and Connecticut to Portland and Berkeley, from Madison to Memphis. Time and distance and life have made shared experiences, and sharing itself, difficult. But as we grow older I think we're looking for things that bind rather than separate, for things that can and should be shared before time and distance and life run their course and opportunity passes.

"When I die," my father said, "I want to be cremated, and I want you boys to put me in the river. And," he added, that bad boy twinkle in his eye, "I want you to take a shot of whiskey when you do it."

We did.

When Dad died, I called a friend, Ham Smythe, who kept a houseboat in the Wolf River Harbor. My brothers and I stepped on board one very early, very cold morning in late January of 1987, Dad's ashes in hand, a bottle of his whiskey, Jim Beam, in my pocket. We rounded the tip of Mud Island and headed upstream fighting heavy current under a heavy winter sky, three brothers at Ham's transom fighting memories.

We heated water on a camp stove and made really atrocious instant coffee. Ham had found a very old jar of it next to a bottle of antifreeze and a can of 3-in-1 oil, either one of which would have tasted better and warmed us up faster. The whiskey was for later.

North of the bridge, several long rock fingers reach out for Harbor Town from the opposite shore, soldiers in the Corps' constant battle against the river. We marked the first and, as we passed it, each of us put Dad in the river. We continued north a bit and then turned back downriver. As we passed again, just the way he wanted, each of us took a long pull from the Beam and said goodbye, each in our own way.

Whatever may separate us, we're bound by that morning and by him, and we are all from this place, part of this place and of him and of each other wherever we are. Whenever I cross the bridge I look to the north, to that azimuth formed by that finger of rock in the river below, and I reset my compass.

My brother's hip is sore, but it's going to be okay, and all three of us are still going fishing next month.

I'm a Memphian, a defining point in the journey we all share.

“Comfort, structure and form can be found in liturgy, and in a jump shot.”

Can I Get An Amen

Regardless of how the playoffs turn out, Memphis has won.

As published April 29, 2011

Glory be.

As the Duke divinity graduate rises and throws up a prayer, an entire city rises with him. All know his name, as he was chosen by them in the beginning and then banished to the wilderness. Well, to Houston anyway. Now he returns. Now he holds their hope. A moment later and ten years coming, we are delivered of our distress in high-def, screaming for joy in front of our TVs. Heaven help us, Shane Battier has ripped a three pointer and the Memphis Grizzlies have won their very first playoff game. Bless their hearts, the San Antonio Spurs have just heard the first lesson in their own house.

Transcendent.

The sinner stands at the center of attention – his only option is himself – and releases it. As it rises, all in the building rise with it. His bruised and purple past are in it, all the ugliness and thuginess in its arc, but when it comes down it is the act of a changed man who pays other people's utility bills, whose talent has electrified us and whose heart has captured ours. All in this congregation are on their feet, joy has erupted, people are dancing in the aisles and, I'm pretty sure, speaking in tongues. All hell has broken loose, Zach Randolph has ripped a three pointer and the Memphis Grizzlies have won their very first playoff game at home. Bless their hearts, but here endeth the second lesson for the West's number one seed.

Redemptive.

God isn't on the Grizzlies bench any more than on the Spurs. Despite all the thanks that come his way in post game interviews, Jesus has never worn one team's sweatshirt or the other, and has caused no blown layups or bricked free throws. Muhammad has never screamed at or questioned the parentage of any referees. Hinduism would not support my belief that Manu Ginobili will come back as a flopping carp. Buddha would not find anything said by either analysts or fans – or Phil Jackson for that matter – to be particularly enlightening.

However, for me anyway, the presence of something larger than our understanding, deeper than our knowing, beyond our explanation can be felt just as much or more in big water, big skies and big weather – and in moments great and small with each other – than in spaces prescribed for it.

Comfort, structure and form can be found in liturgy, and in a jump shot. Joy can be found in a favorite hymn, in a smile or touch, and in the crazed grins of 19,000 people waving towels.

If churches are the most exclusive and segregated places in Memphis on a Sunday morning, FedExForum is the most inclusive and integrated place in Memphis on a Saturday night. Every income, political stripe, racial profile, religious belief, class distinction, address and opinion stand side-by-side united in a celebration of renewed faith in and of a city.

Rejoice and be glad in it.

I'm a Memphian, and I believe.

"Our kids can do anything,
but not if we do nothing."

Building Models

Most of the solutions we're being offered for our various and sundry urban problems seem to have several things in common:

The loudest come from white people over 50 and usually start with, "And I'll tell you another damn thing…"

They are simplistic so as not to strain simple minds.

They are not merely dogmatic, but red-in-the-face, a-little-spit-at-the corner-of-your-mouth dogmatic.

They are based on some time in the past, generally a hybrid of King Arthur's Camelot, Robert Young's "Father Knows Best," and your choice of John Wayne movies.

They are most often voiced with the greatest volume by those with the least knowledge of the subject at hand and the least experience in dealing with or managing it.

So let's get started with this week's column, and I'll tell you another damn thing…

As published May 27, 2011

A 99.6 percent success rate.

We've seen the letters to the editor, heard the guy two stools down, the geniuses spitting into talk show microphones, "It's not the teachers, it's the parents."

If I'm 17 in south Memphis right now, we don't have time to teach or reach my parents to teach or reach me. I have little brothers and sisters I'm responsible for, they're hungry, I'm mad. And I just put a gun in my pocket and walked out the door.

When there's one exhausted parent or no parent at home, where would you have me go? When home is no place I can safely come home to, when the corner is my mentor, the street my support, what would you do with me? When there are thousands of me one meltdown away from you, can you actually pretend that we have nothing to do with each other?

I'm next door. What happens to me tonight when I walk out that door happens to you as a city tomorrow.

The flat earth Tennessee legislature – declaring war on teachers and marching education backwards in lockstep – doesn't get it. People who talk just in terms of what used to be or in terms of 20 years from now – or just talk – don't get it either. We need to stop *these* teen pregnancies, graduate *these* kids, save *this* generation so it can save the next.

We need to stop that kid at that door and open another one right now.

There are people who get it. Alisha Kiner, principal at Booker T. Washington High School, gets it, and the tough love she gives out keeps kids from giving in. Digger Phelps, legendary coach and motivator, gets it, recently telling an audience of prominent Memphis business people to get off their assets and get into a mentoring program. President Obama gets it, coming here for the BTW commencement in recognition of what that amazing inner city class did, raising their grades, raising their graduation rate more than 20 percent, raising the hope of a city, and symbolically through his appearance, the hope of a nation for inner city schools.

There are programs that get it. The Boys & Girls Club, building model citizens from the very raw product of urban reality, gets it.

Half of BTW's graduating class went to the Porter Boys & Girls Club across the street instead of staying on the street. For mentoring and guidance. For role models, reinforcement, and a sense of self-worth. For what can happen when parents can't be there but others are willing and able to step in and stand up.

The graduation rate for Memphis City Schools is in the low sixties. Last year, the Boys & Girls Clubs had a graduation rate of 97.6 percent among the seniors in their six clubs. This year, with three times as many seniors, the graduation rate was 99.6 percent.

Our kids can do anything, but not if we do nothing.

I'm a Memphian, and our kids can inspire Presidents.

“If we don’t remember our
extraordinary shooting stars,
we’re left with just the
ordinary light of day.”

A Memphis Marvel

"I wanted freedom, freedom to indulge in whatever caprice struck my fancy, freedom to search in the farthermost corners of the Earth for the beautiful, the joyous and the romantic."

You go, Richard. You go.

As published June 3, 2011

The real-life adventure serial.

"I'm going to see Halliburton Tower," I told the Rhodes College guard.

"Why?"

Why indeed. On what appear to be the tower's main doors a sign says, ironically, "Please use main door." The tribute to Richard Halliburton that I'm told used to grace the space behind those locked doors has been covered in carpet, now the office of a college vice president. Not only is it difficult to find much evidence of Halliburton in Memphis, you can't find much of him in his own memorial bell tower.

Richard Halliburton wrote a steamer trunk of best sellers and syndicated articles, but to call him merely an author would be like calling Indiana Jones merely an anthropologist. However, while Indy's unbelievable fictional adventures are just that, Halliburton's unbelievable adventures were real. His books had Saturday movie matinee titles like *The Royal Road to Romance, The Glorious Adventure, The Flying Carpet* and *Book of Marvels.* His followers included a maharajah or two, the odd despot, the last Emperor of China, contemporaries like Hemingway and Fitzgerald, and an entire generation of readers. His home is said to be the model for Ayn Rand's "Heller House" in *The Fountainhead.*

Memphis-raised and Princeton-educated, he was never comfortable in traditional roles. Not in how and where he lived. Not in even one minute of his much larger-than-life life. For Halliburton, not just one descent into the Mayan Well of Death would do, so he jumped in twice. Like Lord Byron, he swam the Hellespont. Like Hannibal, he rode an elephant across the Alps. He re-enacted Robinson Crusoe's island ordeal, retraced Cortez's expedition to the heart of the Aztec Empire, and followed Homer's Odyssey and Odysseus across the Mediterranean. He climbed the Matterhorn, was the first to climb Mount Fuji in winter, and stood in the open cockpit of a biplane to photograph Everest while circumnavigating the globe. He lived with the French Foreign Legion, hid by day in the Taj Mahal to swim in the pool by moonlight, and swam the length of the Panama Canal after famously paying the lowest toll in its history for his passage. 36¢. He commissioned The Sea Dragon to be built – a jaunty, 75-foot Chinese junk – to take him from Hong Kong to San Francisco in 1939, and, at age 39, he would go down with her in a typhoon. Like his friend Amelia Earhart, lost at sea.

One of the world's most famous characters in his time, his time was past. Just as that typhoon took him down, the storm of World War II broke over Europe and his unabashed romanticism was as out-of-date as Wordsworth, Coleridge and Byron who inspired it.

The tower was given by his parents, but perhaps his home,

Hangover House in Laguna Beach, is the better symbol of his life – an adventure unto itself, dangling, seemingly suspended, above the Pacific Ocean.

I'm a Memphian, and if we don't remember our extraordinary shooting stars, we're left with just the ordinary light of day.

"I don't fish, and people who do fish talk about fish like this, big enough to inspire tales, bigger still each time the tale is told."

Moby Rainbow

Random good fortune could well be flowing your way. Have a line in the water.

As published June 10, 2011

Lucky catches.

Last week I caught a whale.

The river was too high to catch this fish, far too much trash churned and turned in its brown rush, far too distracting and suspicious for already suspicious rainbow, much less this wily old monster. I can't catch this fish. I don't fish, and people who do fish talk about fish like this, big enough to inspire tales, bigger still each time the tale is told.

When it breaks the surface, the fish and I both know I'm outclassed. It will snap my four-pound line and spit out my ridiculous little hook. It will leave me standing there, dripping defeat in a boat, both of us knowing I'm the one in the Little Red River who doesn't belong.

When it breaks the second time in a blinding, angry flash of sun off scales, I can see in its eye what Ahab (aka: Gregory Peck) must have seen when … okay … maybe I'm getting a little carried away. I'm just saying. This was a big rainbow. A largemouth bass in a trout suit. A brown trout disguised as a rainbow. Seven pan-sized catches in one package.

"Keep the rod up," Mac said from behind me. "Let it run, let it run and wear itself out," Mac, the one in the boat who can fish, advised. And when we did see the fish the first time, Mac, who's seen them all, said quietly, almost reverently, "Don't…lose…this…fish."

I was lucky.

I was lucky to be born and raised in a town with a warm and funky climate that grows creativity even in the cracks of its sidewalks and moves to a beat as palpable as its summer heat. Incredibly lucky when that cute college girl said yes to that first date, and to the rest of our lives. And when our kids were born and when they both came back here after college. And every time they've made me proud, and made me laugh, and made me wonder at the wonder of it.

Mac and I don't know each other well but after this fishing trip we know each other better. In several months, we're going to be grandfathers, sharing a grandbaby. After we netted that tired, proud fish, measured, weighed, and photographed it, Mac took it from me and carefully lowered it into the water, holding its mouth upstream against the current, and watching the gills. "Breathe, sweetheart, breathe," he said, and he held it until it did and he could return it to the river. That's a good gene pool to share.

Looks like I'm lucky again.

Folks around here spend way too much time on what went under and what got away, and not nearly enough on what's coming and what's just under the surface. The current in Memphis is stronger than it's been in years. Go catch something.

By the way, that bad boy was 21 inches long and 7 1/2 pounds.

I'm a Memphian, and I fish in lucky waters.

"If the past is our measure of success, we'll be history."

Coal. Ice. And Coca-Cola.

If we consider the present to be a permanent condition, we'll be wrong tomorrow. If the past is our measure of success, we'll be history.

Whether we choose to move backward or forward, the power is ours.

As published August 19, 2011

The power of vision.

Many families have a story about opportunities missed, fortunes lost.

My great uncle was in the retail coal and ice business in Memphis. Around 1907, our story goes, a woman owed him about $7,500 – a piece of change then. She couldn't repay him according to the terms set, so she offered something she owned instead to cover the debt. He turned her down but gave her new terms and she eventually paid off the loan. When asked to justify his decision (and he was asked a lot), he infamously replied, "What she had was a passing fancy, a temporary infatuation no one really needs. People will always need coal and ice."

What she had, what he turned down, was the Coca-Cola franchise for this part of the world. The telling of that story often requires a stiff drink, and it's not Coca-Cola.

This city, famous for inventing so many things, for giving the world a beat to dance to, should never be content to sit on the stoop while the world goes by, waiting for the ice man to drop a block off from his wagon or listening for the rattle of the coal going down the basement chute.

We need to get our assets moving forward.

Power, for instance.

Right out there in Hickory Hill, Sharp is making solar panels. Right now. Right here. The question isn't whether or not the world wants solar panels – they're hotter than Halle Berry – it's why in the world we don't see them all over Memphis rooftops, all over anything facing south in inventive, creative applications to show viability and versatility.

Right in front of us, this country's greatest river rolls by, deep and free-flowing, at a steady clip of seven or eight miles per hour. 24/7/365, 366 in a leap year. Turbines, either riverbed mounted or suspended from barges, can turn that river current into electrical current. The question isn't how – that's known – the question is why the hell we aren't on this like hot on August, doing whatever is necessary – and I mean whatever – to make sure those turbines spin right here, are made right here.

Creative power from Memphis. Green and sustainable. Green like money. No dead dinosaurs required. No offshore drilling. No price per barrel. No Mideast wars.

If the city, Sharp and Bass Pro Shop would bait the south side of The Pyramid with solar panels, all three would haul more business and positive publicity into our collective boat than Bill Dance on steroids. And all of us would feel the power.

All we have to do is let the sun shine on new ideas.

If we spin our incentives and cover the river bottom with turbines, the electricity we generate could shock the country. And all of us would find new energy.

All we have to do is go with the flow.

Or we can stick with coal and ice.

I'm a Memphian, and it's time to get fired up and plugged in.

"Life should be about taking responsibility, and about leaving a campsite, or wherever you've been, better than you found it."

Everyday Heroes

"An act demonstrating exceptional character that reflects an uncommon degree of concern for the well-being of others."

What a young man did in Germantown a couple of weeks ago reminded me of those words, and of a couple of events I was involved with 20 years ago when I first saw them.

It also reminded me to keep the faith that the best in us will prevail.

As published September 23, 2011

Be prepared. We need heroes every day.

The assistant scoutmaster beside me was asking about procedure if something appeared to be broken. "Don't do nothing," answered the earnest, doubly negative instructor, "Transport."

"What if it's a compound fracture?" "Don't do nothing," came the reply, "Transport." Someone else asked about tourniquets, and was told – all together now – "Don't do nothing. Transport."

And so it went.

We were participants in a Boy Scout adult leadership course 20 years ago, and fear of failure, or blame, or litigation, or all of the above was beginning to guide official policy and taking responsibility was becoming synonymous with taking unnecessary risk.

It seemed that the motto of "Be Prepared" was being replaced with "Don't do nothing. Transport." In the larger context of today's me-first society, if confronted with something unpleasant, challenging, even scary, don't deal with it, send it somewhere else. Not my problem.

If Jeremy Palazolo and Igor Kobas – and this may be a triple negative – didn't "don't do nothing," people would have died.

Jeremy Palazolo was a scout in Troop 34. On a 1992 camping trip, his group came upon a young woman wandering in the woods babbling about a boyfriend and a cliff. While others took off to find a ranger, Jeremy and scout dad C.B. Jolley took off to find the boyfriend. They did – in shock, bleeding from everywhere, and on top of a waterfall he'd already fallen off of once and was about to fall off of again. Using his first aid training and pieces of his and C.B.'s clothing, Jeremy treated the boyfriend for shock, stopped the bleeding, and, according to what rangers told me later, probably saved the young man's life. The Boy Scouts gave Jeremy their Medal Of Merit, honoring an act "demonstrating exceptional character that reflects an uncommon degree of concern for the well-being of others." Jeremy was all of 15 at the time. And exceptional indeed.

He didn't think what he did was a big deal.

I don't know if Igor Kobas was a scout, but what he did is what being prepared is all about. A couple of weeks ago, faced with a young man bleeding out, with the ambulance trapped on the other side of the train that had just severed his leg, with the onlookers either screaming or on cell phones or both, Igor whipped off his belt, tied off the wound, and gave that young man the chance to become an old one. I don't know what recognition Igor will receive, but we should all recognize what a positive difference calm, reasoned response can make in the midst of crisis and hysteria. Igor is all of 21. And exceptional indeed.

After the ambulance pulled away, Igor walked back across the street and finished his valet parking shift at Elfo's.

In this old scoutmaster's opinion, a lot of scouting, and life, should be about taking responsibility, and about leaving a campsite, or wherever you've been, better than you found it.

I'm a Memphian, and Jeremy and Igor make us better.

“They were just games, but games can bring out the best and worst in us.”

Remembering The Decathlon

Never mind that we can't remember who competed, we can't remember who won the silver and bronze. We're not even sure who won the gold.

But, ah, the games. We remember the games.

As published August 3, 2012

Shooting the moon for gold.

My fellow decathlete, Jeff Chamblin, called. We remember the competition as if it were yesterday.

Surely we all remember the wedge on 18 at Galloway, dug from a heavy lie in a front yard on Walnut Grove, having arrived there after a 350-yard drive, 250 yards of that by virtue of bounces in the street. Even now, we can see the wedge rising over five lanes of traffic. We can hear the horns, the homeowner scream from his porch, as we watch that scarred, bruised warrior of a ball hit, bounce and bite to eight feet for birdie. Don't tell me about the troublesome rules of golf. In this competition, if you could find it and hit it, it was in play, and that was a helluva shot.

We all gasped as one when top right English sent the three into the seven across the table to drop the money ball into the corner pocket. We couldn't believe it when the backhand slam from somewhere out in the driveway cleared the net and sent the favorite diving into the corner of the carport, waving his paddle at air, as a ping pong ball and his medal chances whizzed by his ear.

In the middle of the London Olympics in 2012, the Memphis Olympics in the middle of 1970 come to mind.

You see, Jeff and I worked for *The Commercial Appeal* that summer and while we were supposed to be selling ads one afternoon, we were doing something more rewarding – drinking beer and coming up with a decathlon of the games we grew up playing – a sort of east Memphis upbringing Olympiad, if you will.

Horse was in, Around The World was out, because Horse is more creative since you don't shoot from fixed positions. Another beer. Poker and Hearts were in, but Bridge was out since a partner is required. Monopoly was on board but Parcheesi was, well, too cheesy. Another beer. Leftfield ball and bowling would be the team sports. And so on. And another beer.

Ten competitors. Ten events over the weekend. Bowling, Leftfield Ball, Horse, 9-Ball, Golf, Tennis, Poker, Ping Pong, Monopoly, Hearts.

We remember as if it were yesterday. Except we can't remember everybody who competed, or what we competed for – beer and money to be sure, but we're not sure how much. Jeff claims he took the gold, but I know better.

In the last event – Hearts – I had the queen of spades, and the ace and queen of hearts, and when I took Jeff's king with that ace, I shot the moon and used the 26 points to take him and the gold.

At least that's what I remember. I think.

They were just games, but games can bring out the best and worst in us, show us some of our brightest and darkest moments, stir old memories, and cause 20 minutes of belly laughs between two old friends on the phone.

That's pure gold.

I'm a Memphian, and I love the Olympics.

"Lately, kinetic energy is blowing across long-still ground, and it's enough to give you heart."

The Heart Beats

I believe there is such a thing as romantic realism – being in love with what's possible in the here and now to make the when and then a better place to be.

I further believe that nostalgia for nostalgia's sake, a longing to live in a time long gone and shaped by selective memory, to be largely an old fart exercise. Like the alcohol that generally fuels it, it's best taken in moderation and not taken too seriously. Too much of it just makes your head hurt and makes you less able to deal with the day in front of you.

However, using the past to inform the future – respecting, re-shaping and reusing its ghosts to provide new spirit in the present and bringing new life to old haunts – can really get your heart going.

As published September 14, 2012

The heart beats. Again.

A lifetime ago, screwdrivers with lifetime guarantees came from an art moderne castle, and screwdrivers with orange juice came from the only other Friday's outside of Manhattan.

Ben-Hur, Spartacus and Lawrence of Arabia came from Crosstown, and big splashes came from the Fairgrounds.

Before Home Depot, Best Buy and big boxes, the biggest box of all – the 1.5 million square feet and 14-story tower of Sears & Roebuck – towered over Crosstown Memphis. The stuff of dreams was delivered one lawnmower, one refrigerator, one pair of pants, one screwdriver at a time over what seemed like a thousand counters or from a loading dock that seemed – no, wait – *was* a hundred yards long. My grandmother took me to see big movies on Crosstown Theatre's big screen in the shadow of Sears, and Nora and I held our first house together with the baling wire, chewing gum and advice we got in the basement hardware department.

Before you could get a drink or a glass of wine outside of a private club or a brown bag, a few Memphis twenty-somethings poured themselves a double-shot of chutzpah and went to New York to talk the owners of hot spot T.G.I. Friday's into letting them open one here. And the party started in Overton Square.

Before there were pools outside of private clubs, before you knew anybody with one in the backyard, you got on the bus, on your bike or on your Keds and rode them to the Fairgrounds to jump in the water with everybody else.

That was a lifetime ago, before much of the heart of Memphis was left for dead.

But Sears stirs. The Church Health Center, St. Jude, ALSAC, Methodist Healthcare and the West Clinic are bringing hope, healing and warmth to that long-cold monument of neglect. Crosstown Arts, Gestalt Community Schools, Rhodes College, Memphis Teacher Residency, and a team of architects and planners are shining light into its long-dark corners so that we might clearly see all that's possible.

Overton Square rises. In an innovative public/private partnership, the city and Loeb Properties are cleaning up, dressing up and stepping out to throw the party again. And we're all invited.

The Fairgrounds has a pulse. Right on top of the old pool, The Salvation Army is making a much bigger splash. In January, they'll open The Kroc Center, 15 acres and 100,000 square feet of more than you can imagine. More than a multipurpose center, this is the new center of the city.

Recently, a bright "Beacon" rose above the grassy triangle across from old Sears Crosstown. With the kind of shared creative spirit that makes anything possible, Harry Freeman and Sara Ratner made the sculpture possible, and artists Eli Gold and Colin Kidder made their vision from bicycle wheels. When the wind blows, the wheels turn and catch the light in refreshing new ways.

Lately, kinetic energy is blowing across long-still ground, and it's enough to give you heart.

I'm a Memphian, and I can feel the beat.

“Food fuels stories.”

Story On The Side

Many of you have responded to this year's Tasteful List column not just in confirmation or rejection of the choices, not just with suggested additions or corrections, but with what those things meant to you and mean to you now.

Food fuels stories.

For instance, every time I smell onion rings, I can see a mountain of them at the Pig 'n Whistle, and I can see movies at Lowe's Palace, parties at Clearpool, and dark places to park.

But that's another story.

As published September 21, 2012

A story in every bite.

As I listened, I remembered comedian David Brenner discussing directions in the South. He noted that directions come with a story, and they may include turn left at the three-legged dog, and that everything comes with grits.

The teller this time was friend Hal – world traveler, retired pilot, former Tiger lineman and current gourmand. The subject was my recent column on recommended things to chew on around here, but not really. That was just the skillet grease to get the stories fired up.

"When you're about ten minutes out of Walnut," Hal said, assuming everybody not only knows where Walnut is, but also when they're ten minutes out, "just give the Express Shop #17 a call and they'll throw some chicken livers on the grill." He then paused, simply nodded twice, and you knew that was as good as it gets. "And," he rebooted, "look for the guy on the shoulder of Highway 7 around Abbeville, got him an oil drum grill and a plastic sign that says 'Ribs.' Lord, Lord. Here I am, driving to Oxford with a pile of pig and aluminum foil in my lap, throwing bones out the window and laughing out loud. I swear that was better than the five-star New York restaurant I was in the night before."

As any good reviewer will tell you, it's not just food; it's presentation and ambience.

A while back, headed home and hungry, I saw the South Parkway exit in my headlights, almost the driveway to the original Coletta's, home to the original barbecue pizza. I ordered one to go, and asked for a beer while I waited. They directed me to the bar. The bar? I'd been coming to Coletta's since Caesar came to Gaul and I'd never noticed a bar, but there it was down the hall, a walk past the bathrooms right into somewhere around 1963. In an instant, you knew that all the people in there knew each other, knew exactly what was right and wrong with the world – and didn't know you. They were all sizes and colors, both sexes, and aged somewhere between early middle age and early Jurassic.

"Draft's two-for-one," the bartender said. "That's Harry's seat," somebody else said. "Shut up, Moose," the bartender said, "Harry's not here." "How about some baloney?" yet another voice questioned. I turned and there, holding a big pan of savory, was the man I'd seen cooking something outside when I pulled in. "Can't have mine," Moose said. The restaurant couldn't have it either. It was the bar's and not for sale.

Over the course of two beers – remember, two-for-one – I learned that one night every week (I'm not telling which one or they'll come after me) a different bar regular cooked for the rest. I hope they still do.

Might be ribs or chicken, catfish or chicken livers. Or it might be barbecued, blackened and blissful baloney – the stuff of good stories.

I'm a Memphian, and the number for Express Shop #17 is 662.223.6399.

"One day, it's all beautiful. The next day, it all turns to crap. Or maybe that's not the message at all."

Ginkgos and Band-Aids

Happy Thanksgiving, y'all.

As published November 23, 2012

Look for the wonder. Repeat.

Right outside my window is a female ginkgo tree, her boyfriend is on the other side of the house, and every fall they engage in an ancient mating dance, a spectacular competition for attention. So exhausting is the effort, it doesn't last long. So intense is the result, it's explosive. And then it's gone, leaving only a memory.

One morning they're both green. That afternoon they're a bit less green. Overnight, they turn. The next morning, they shed light, a brilliant yellow that doesn't so much stop you as arrest you, so bright it shines through window shades and burns off gloom, a yellow that turns every other yellow green.

And the next day, it seems, it's all gone. Their leaves fall as one, leaving the host naked and alone, covering the patio and everything on it with their loss.

"Watch your step out there," Nora said. "The dogs just left a message in the ginkgo leaves and I got it."

So it goes. One day, it's all beautiful. The next day, it all turns to crap. Or maybe that's not the message at all.

My immediate family has been visited by death, near death and deadly threat, by deceit and heartbreak, by cancer in varying form, by Alzheimer's and plain old dementia, by diabetes, alcoholism, kidney disease and kidney stones, emphysema, bankruptcy, divorce, blown dreams and blue toe, broken bones and torn muscles, curved spines and fractured vertebrae, stupid mistakes and senseless loss, rejection and reflux, gum disease, blood disease and general disease.

And that's just up to now. And I'm due for a check-up.

But we've also been visited by each other, by shared experience and gained appreciation, by children and grandchildren, by a lot of friends and a lot of delightful silliness, by unforgettable moments and uncontrolled laughter, by faith and hope, and love. And by waking up today.

We've been visited by the privilege of life, the gift of perception, and the opportunity of choice.

Last weekend, the one-year-old was bleeding on several adults and three dogs, on everything and everybody, as she screamed her way around the big room. The very tip of her index finger had been nipped by errant fingernail clippers and she was a fountain of misery. A bit later, she was wearing her very first Band-Aid and a very big smile as she held it up high and waddled across the same room to proudly show it to her grandfather.

All better now.

The ginkgo trees are regarded as living fossils, literally writing their history in stone dating back almost 300 million years, some claiming to live more than 2,500 years. And they've done that dance every one of those years a few billion times around the world, and right outside my window. To see the wonder of it, I only need to look.

The ginkgo trees don't leave you with a memory, they leave you with the promise of their return.

I'm a Memphian, and, this week, I'm especially thankful.

“Good teachers light a fire.”

Olds Flames

Some say it should be all about the kids, others say the teachers. What it shouldn't be all about is courtrooms and churches, buildings and boundaries and boards, real estate values and sales taxes, yours and mine, them and us.

It should be about the recognition in all those faces, the light coming on in all those eyes, the dawning and nurturing of knowledge.

It should be all about the kids. And the teachers.

As published November 30, 2012

Teachers, not schools, teach.

If you're wondering how many pieces of notebook paper it takes to produce a truly impressive spitball, it's ten, give or take.

Terry was occupying most of the rear corner, busily inserting one piece of notebook paper after another into his mouth. Known for both gross weight and behavior, Terry was larger and older than us; the former the result of being so fond of everything in the cafeteria that he went back again and again, and the latter the result of being so fond of several grades that he went back for those, too.

Mrs. Olds was writing something on the board as Terry removed and shaped the massive mess of a missile from his mouth and launched it. It struck the board with a wet, slippery thud just left of her head. Before the gasp of the class faded, with one smooth move, Mrs. Olds swept the eraser from the ledge, spun on her left foot, planted her right, and delivered a spinning, chalk-dust-spitting frozen rope right between the wide eyes of the amazed Terry. She knew where it had come from, and she knew how to return the favor. He wore that amazed expression all the way to the school office. He may still wear the mark.

Rosemary Olds left a mark.

That throw alone assures her of permanent coolness, but she was cooler than that. She knew some weird and wonderful people, and she introduced us. To Coleridge, his Ancient Mariner and that dead bird around his neck. To the Shelleys, both the precious Percy and the monstrous Mary. To Byron and the Brontë girls. To the brooding Faulkner, his bear and Emily's rose. To a whole world of carefully chosen words, made immortal by their choice.

Double, double toil and trouble;
Fire burn, and caldron bubble.

We heard it first, a low growl from the back of the dark room. The lights were off and the blinds drawn when we'd entered and found our desks – whispering as you do in the dark, and then going quiet as you do when you hear something dark.

Double, double toil and trouble;
Fire burn, and caldron bubble.

Louder now. Closer. A kind of cackle, a very cold kind. A hunched and hooded figure moved through the room, turning one hand over the other, repeating the dark words over and over, louder and louder.

Double, double toil and trouble;
Fire burn, and caldron bubble.

And the figure flipped the light switch and all the girls screamed – okay – we all screamed. The figure was, of course, Mrs. Olds, the hood was her raincoat, and that was her introduction to Shakespeare's Macbeth and his witches.

Rosemary Olds lit a fire.

Good teachers light a fire. How long and bright it burns depends on the source of the fuel, but if it's never lit in the first place, life can be a bleak journey indeed.

I'm a Memphian, and I'd like to thank Mrs. Olds, and good teachers everywhere, for the light.

"Isolated and ignored, armed and angry, we perish."

New Heroes

This week, the kids of Sandy Hook Elementary will return to their desks, surrounded by familiar things, warm and supportive and innocent things – things transported from cold, dark reality to a place where they might again see the sun, see the light, in classrooms recreated in hope.

As published January 4, 2013
Some references came from a post on
The Hartford Courant website, December 22, 2012

School lessons in heroism.

On Friday morning, December 21 – one week after semi-automatic gunfire swept through elementary school classrooms and the nation, murdering innocence – one week after a Memphis police officer stood between a bullet and you and me, giving us all she had – a single two-ton bell in the tower of Idlewild Presbyterian Church rang 29 times. Once for officer Martoiya Lang, twenty times for the children of Newtown, six times for their teachers and, unlike anywhere else I'm aware of, once for the shooter's mother and once for him. Each is the toll of madness, of misplaced priorities and violence, of the belief that more armed violence is not only a righteous solution but a constitutional right. And of a country where it's easier to buy an assault rifle than vote, easier to buy ammunition than Sudafed.

But in the midst of the wringing of hands, gnashing of teeth, and loud calls for immediate remedy that follow tragic events, there are quieter heroes and quieter lessons about how to live in communion with each other.

In this new year, I have new heroes and hope in the face of horror: Steve Vavrek, James Agostine, and 500 locksmiths, plumbers, electricians, and neighbors in Monroe, Connecticut, who volunteered to work 24 hours a day to turn one of their empty schools into a school for the Sandy Hook kids in neighboring Newtown. They didn't simply provide space, they converted a middle school into an elementary school to code, raising bathroom floors so urinals would be low enough, lowering all the handrails to be low enough, painting the walls in Sandy Hook's colors, and jumping over bureaucratic barriers to do it all in days, not months, getting the governor to get government out of the way.

And they sent semis eight miles north to Newtown to retrieve the innocent world of Sandy Hook school and put it back in place. Little desks and chairs, globes and maps, drawings on the doors and windows, posters on the walls. They brought the school mascot, a turtle named Shelley, to live in the library. Just as it should be.

They're not charging Newtown a penny. You're my new hero, Monroe.

"They're going to come back, and if little Chaz had a desk near the window, he'll have the same desk by the window," said Monroe first selectman, Steve Vavrek. You're my new hero, Steve.

When I first heard of this, a blip on CNN amid all the cloying coverage and emotional sledgehammers we were all hit with that first awful weekend, I saw James Agostine, superintendent of schools in Monroe, being interviewed. He was doing fine, until he mentioned having to adjust all the toilet heights because, pausing as tears welled up, this was being done for little people. You're my new hero, James.

Together, with common purpose and common sense, we can survive. Isolated and ignored, armed and angry, we perish.

I'm a Memphian, and, to paraphrase poet John Donne, the bell tolls for all of us.

"The first lesson is you can't get past reality and get anywhere real."

1955

The past fascinates, informs and challenges. What actually happened there, and why, can also confuse, irritate and be pretty inconvenient. That's why we very often turn the past into nostalgic journeys to pleasant places. Nothing wrong with that if that's your trip, unless you start to believe the tripping is reality.

For instance, Texas has rewritten the past to suit their present political purposes and called that fiction fact in the schools' history books.

The past has much to teach us. The first lesson is you can't get past reality and get anywhere real.

As published August 20, 2010

Learn. Don't return.

I swear by my Roy Rogers chuckwagon, if just one more Boomer emails me about going back to the terrific 50s, I'm going to upchuck. Then I'm going to freeze up your AC, microwave your 45s, throw a rotary-dial phone through your flat screen, cancel your cell, and … very first thing … gag your Google.

No, those little paraffin Coke bottles with the sugar swamp water in them weren't terrific, and neither was watching Perry Como in fuzzy pastels and everything else in black-and-white. Those were just new things, things that aren't around anymore because things got better.

No, sweating through Memphis summers sucking attic fan air through bug-covered screens wasn't a charming memory, a toughen-up exercise, or a life lesson. It was just hot. Can't breathe, can't move, somebody-turn-on-the-sprinkler hot.

Okay … yes … the 1955 T-bird was terrific.

The reason you thought everything was terrific in 1955? **YOU WERE FIVE YEARS OLD.**

In the summer of 1955, I believed in Santa Claus, Elvis was dating the girl next door, I had just learned how to whistle, and I was starting the first grade. It was terrific. **I WAS FIVE YEARS OLD.**

My parents, on the other hand, were getting over McCarthy, contemplating a bomb shelter in the back yard, figuring out what to do without Mr. Crump doing everything, and raising three kids in my grandmother's house.

The city they lived in was actually two cities, one black and one white, and they no more shared their lives and opportunities than they shared their schools, restaurants, water fountains or public bathrooms.

And in the backyard hammock, they could feel the post-war breeze as Atlanta blew by taking the lead from us as the South's major city.

In 1980, I merged my ad agency with another in order to survive and the economy was taking a double-digit beating in the "misery index," but our daughter was a star in senior kindergarten. Life was terrific. In 1986, I started a new business and put everything we had at risk, but our son hit his very first home run playing T-ball. Life was terrific. **THEY WERE FIVE YEARS OLD.**

Nostalgia, always positive and selective, can be fun and comforting. It can't be a destination. Don't long to go where you can't go, long to make where you're going better.

In 1955 and now, Memphis was and is loaded with potential. Then and now, Memphis should have and still can serve as a model for the whole country in addressing diversity and unity. Looking back for what we might learn from the things we can still love and celebrate, and from the mistakes we made, can help fuel our way forward. Actually going back just puts us behind.

As a Billy Joel lyric reflected, "The good ole days weren't all that good, and tomorrow's not as bad as it seems." Let's make tomorrow terrific.

I'm a Memphian, and I remember Merrymobiles. Now, let's just please get on with it.

"Before there was the Titanic,
there was the Sultana."

Dead Reckoning

You would think if the biggest something that's ever happened – in a category of pretty big somethings – blew up practically in front of you, you'd remember something like that.

You'd think.

As published April 6, 2012

Ghost of a river.

Jimmy Ogle is a Memphis history savant. He knows things about people and places around here that even those people didn't know in the first place.

Going somewhere with Jimmy is a trip.

The other day, Jimmy navigated and I handled my car's tiller across a 30-mile-wide lake – on dry land. I plowed upstream in the main channel of the Mississippi – in a plowed field. In the surreal light of fire on water, I wove my way through hundreds already dead and heard the desperate screams of hundreds still alive – as I passed the water features and faux Georgian facades of a brand-new subdivision. In the dusty reality of today's all-but-forgotten Mound City, I remembered that day's Mound City and its citizens throwing together rafts to save all the souls they could. I saw her go down, a spectacular tragedy at the end of a spectacularly tragic war, her fiery gunwales disappearing – 40 feet below a farmer's field. I steered to the landing at Marion, a bustling Mississippi port – and parked my car in front of a still Southern swamp.

It was a late afternoon in March, but Jimmy and I were spending quality time with the ghosts of an early morning in April of 1865.

Before the levees, the river was 30 miles wide this time of year, perhaps but ankle deep in places but all wet. Then, the channel north of the Desoto Bridge was the Tennessee Chute, choked with sandbars. Then, the chute we now see against the river's west bank was the main channel, sweeping six-plus miles west and then north, placing Mound City and Marion on the Mississippi.

Before there was the Titanic, there was the Sultana.

The Titanic carried 2,229 when she hit that iceberg. The Sultana had a capacity of only 376, but carried 2,300 when her boiler exploded, igniting the dawn off Marion, visible from Memphis eight miles south.

The Titanic lost 1,517, capturing the attention of the world then and even now. The Sultana lost at least 1,700, the greatest maritime disaster in American history, and she couldn't even capture a regional headline. Her news was lost in the wave of mourning for Abraham Lincoln, awash in the gunshots that killed his assassin the day before.

She carried the weak and wasted human detritus of war, Union prisoners heading home after somehow surviving the infamy of Andersonville only to die in hot, bright flames or beneath cold, dark water. Where their hope sank, where there was once a great river, a great tragedy and a singular marker in the nation's history and ours, that place should be properly marked and always remembered.

Folks in Marion and around the country – Jimmy introduced me to a few – are determined to do just that. They know if you travel the road that once was a river and stop and listen, you can hear bits and pieces of 2,300 stories washed away by a forgotten current.

I'm a Memphian, and Jimmy and I see ghosts.

"Equal respect for those
who guide you to your seat and
those whose talent stands you
straight up from it."

Stages

I sometimes like to sit in the back of empty theaters and empty churches and listen to the quiet.

There's a presence in both places, a purpose, a promise. There are stages, sets, props.

Both have the potential to inspire and instruct, but also to alienate. To delight, but also to disappoint. To rise, but also to fall.

And both depend on the interaction of those down front with those assembled before them, and all with each other, to determine what will happen in this space.

It's not just the script. It's the interpretation.

Break a leg, Memphis.

As published August 26, 2011

Live applause.

All are in the cast, all responsible for the experience, and all of us have a lot to show for it.

The lines may be drawn on a two-by-four to guide a saw instead of spoken on stage to guide an audience. The song might be whistled to accompany a hammer instead of sung to accompany a chorus. Equal parts sewing needles and director needling. Equal props for props and performances. Equal respect for those who guide you to your seat and those whose talent stands you straight up from it.

Community theater is a community enterprise everywhere. In Memphis, it's a legacy.

Starting in the 1920s and for decades, the Memphis Little Theatre – what would become Theatre Memphis – performed on a stage set in the deep end of Clarence Saunders' never-used Pink Palace indoor swimming pool with the audience stacked up toward the shallow end. It was so tight in there that you had to go outside to turn around and if somebody in the audience coughed, it sounded scripted.

Yet they tended to drown everybody in regional and national play competitions, becoming one of the country's most recognized community theaters, twice representing the United States internationally.

In their own building since 1975, Theatre Memphis has watched the curtain and the economy continue to go up and down for 92 seasons – our shared fortunes rising and falling with each new act – and the show goes on.

Their fired-up executive producer, Debbie Litch, has more energy than the stage lights and a smile that competes for attention with the sequins and feathers she loves to wear. She could get a budget increase from the Tea Party. Their costume designer, André Bruce Ward, is to community theatre what Edith Head is to film. He could make me look good in a Speedo – okay, in anything but a Speedo. The professional staff and 600-plus volunteers do magic things every few weeks and turn plain boards and black boxes into other worlds for us to visit.

And Theatre Memphis is not alone.

Playhouse On The Square – professional in name but very much of this community – has taken abandoned music halls and movie houses and created great theater there out of baling wire, chewing gum, duct tape and the enormous heart of Jackie Nichols for 40 years, and has now raised the curtain on a brand-new, state-of-the-art theater.

Doctors, lawyers and candlestick makers by day play new roles by night at the Germantown Community Theatre, the Harrell Theatre, and the Desoto Family Theatre. Voices Of The South, Hattiloo Theatre and TheatreWorks experiment, stretch and challenge us to see, hear and feel in new ways.

And still more. On our college campuses, in our churches and neighborhoods, in our community centers and school auditoriums. Live theater is more alive in Memphis than in cities several times our size.

And if you don't think The Orpheum involves local actors, you've never seen Pat Halloran pitch season tickets.

And the show is for us.

I'm a Memphian, and local theater gets a standing ovation.

"No one and nothing is irrelevant along the way."

Note to Self

"I'm going to sit right down and write myself a letter."

Fats Waller first made it a hit in 1935. Since then, it's been covered by everybody from Frank Sinatra, Bing Crosby, Dean Martin and Nat King Cole to Bill Haley and the Comets and Scatman Cruthers to Willie Nelson and, alas, Barry Manilow.

It's a very popular song. And it's a very good idea.

Feel free to hum along as you read this week's column.

As published October 7, 2011

We need advice, from ourselves.

About 25 years ago, I closed up my parents' home at the end of their lives. Wandering through the empty house and the memories, I found myself in my old room, going through my desk drawers one more time. In the back of one, way back there, I found something I'd missed – a magnifying glass with a loose handle. Curious, I pulled the handle off and saw a piece of a paper inside. Unrolling it, I instantly recognized the note and laughed out loud, returning that sound to a place once filled with it, replacing a sense of loss with a sense of perspective.

The note said, "Curious son of a bitch aren't you?" Written by me in the eighth grade, planted in a loose handle to catch somebody, and catching only me all those years later.

Thirteen years ago, I took part in The Academy Leadership Intensive, a four-day, heavy lifting exercise of turning yourself inside out in front of 30 or so other folks, and then spotting them while they do the same. At the end, you know a great deal more about yourself and others, and a great deal more about observing, understanding, and the capacity to lead. As part of the process, you're asked to write yourself a letter, telling yourself a thing or two about what matters, to be sent to you months later to check your progress against your own standards.

The other day, Nora and I were cleaning out closet crypts, and – along with the present you didn't give somebody last year or ten years ago and that shirt/suit/coat/blouse/box you know you have but can't find – we found that letter.

I think it still stands up, and I'm still trying to stand up to it. See what you think.

> "Dear Dan,
>
> Remember, always, true vision is not possible with blinders, progress cannot be achieved without motion and that even a little change requires a little chaos. *Create it from time to time.*
>
> You are not in charge of the process or of another single living creature. You are part of the process, and you have considerable impact on others and they on you. *Study each other.*
>
> No one and nothing is irrelevant along the way. *Learn from everything.*
>
> Laughter is free but the cost of not using it is immeasurable. *Humor yourself and others.*
>
> If you're always busy being heard you never hear.

For God's sake, Dan, listen.

No love is unconditional, nor respect unearned, no result guaranteed. *Give back gladly, gleefully, to those who give to you, and be glad for them.*

The condition for love is to give it back. To earn respect, invest in some for others. To achieve results, look for and employ your strengths and the strengths of others.

People are, thank God, different. *Celebrate the differences, challenge sameness.*

Most of all, enjoy the trip without hurting any of the other passengers.

Did I mention listen?"

I'm a Memphian, and somebody just reminded me of things that matter.

“He made it personal, and that makes it last a lifetime.”

Personal Hook

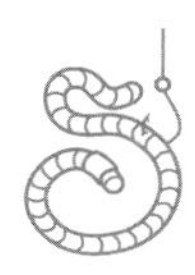

I still tell the story.

About a university president who somehow kept up with thousands of students before computers could do it, who followed their progress before Twitter could do it, who talked to them face-to-face before Facebook pretended to do it, who invited them into his home socially every week to network with each other and faculty before social networks claimed to do it.

About a Memphian, via Milan, who cleaned fish and told jokes in a frat house kitchen to 20 guys, and when he looked at any one of them, he turned 25,000 students into one.

He made it personal, and that makes it last a lifetime.

From an article in Tennessee Alumnus, January, 2012

Caught for life.

At five o'clock on a Sunday morning in 1969 the phone in the frat house rang.

For those of you not familiar with five o'clock on a Sunday morning in a frat house, just think of a graveyard, except that the residents of a graveyard are more likely to be up and about. If the phone rings, it's a wrong number, bad news, or somebody calling for bail money.

This call was for me. "This had better be good," I thought, meaning that the news had better be so bad, the urgency so compelling, that my stumbling down the stairs to the beat of my head would be warranted.

"Daniel? Or is it Danny or Dan?" said the voice. "This is Andy Holt."

Andy Holt. He had the physical profile of a 1952 Pontiac Chieftain hood ornament, and the legendary profile of a tireless champion of both public education and educators. He had ears big enough, with a gentle breeze behind them, to push a boat down the Tennessee River, and a vision big enough, with a gentle spirit behind it, to push a university to integrate, to start a Space Institute, to triple student enrollment and double faculty size. His voice was equal parts molasses and grits, his wit sharp enough to shave with, and his personality warm enough to take the chill out of anybody or any room. He was a speaker and storyteller so mythically gifted, he could open both the minds and wallets of state and federal legislators. As in Dr. Andrew D. Holt. As in President of the University of Tennessee. On my frat house phone. Talking to me.

"Yeah, right," I coughed through the bale of cotton behind my teeth. "Who the hell is this?"

"Wake up, son. This is Andy Holt and we're going fishing. I'll pick you up in 15 minutes."

Andy Holt made it his business to meet as many students as he could. He would host faculty and students at his house – weekly. He would ferry weary students up The Hill on his way to the office. And if he already knew your family, he would make it a point to spend some time with you before you graduated. During his salad days as a teacher and administrator at the West Tennessee State Teachers College, now the University of Memphis, he became a close friend of both my Godfather and one of my uncles.

I didn't know that, but Andy Holt did. So 15 minutes after I hung up the phone, found a pair of jeans in the third pile on the right and made it out onto the porch, he docked a battleship of a Buick out front, threw open the door, handed me a bacon sandwich and set sail for some pond somewhere in west Knoxville.

We sat on the bank of that pond and caught, give or take, three million bream. They were standing in line. We talked about my family, about football, about Vietnam, about girls, about raising chickens and changing majors and the Grateful Dead. We didn't talk about Andy Holt. And we laughed. A lot.

Then, in what was already a remarkable morning, he did something remarkable.

He drove me back to the house, grabbed the big cooler full of fish, and told me to wake everybody up and meet him in the kitchen. In the next hour or so he taught the 20 or so zombies I was able to raise how to clean fish, how to tell a good story, and how to make an impression that lasts a lifetime.

He wasn't a university president, former national president of the NEA or Columbia Ph.D. He was Andy from Milan, hanging with some buddies.

That magic morning, when he looked at any of us, he turned the 25,000 students on campus into one. And every one in that kitchen supports the university to this day and always will.

And we tell the story.

I'm a Memphian, and I've been fishing with Andy Holt.

“When I was little, I was pretty sure you went to cool weddings by horseback.”

Horseback Rides With Weddings

Happy Anniversary to my girls and Happy New Year to all of you.

As published December 28, 2012

Bridal paths.

When I was little, I was pretty sure you went to cool weddings by horseback.

After all, Roy and Dale were married, and they sang "Happy Trails To Us" from the back of a horse every week. Mom and Dad were married, and they spent the first year of their marriage in Arizona riding horses and doing cool-sounding things like punching cattle, shooting rattlesnakes and smoking Old Golds.

And there was that trail right down the middle of the East Parkway median that connected two of the coolest places in my world – the Mid-South Fairgrounds and Overton Park – that Mom told me was called a bridle path.

I'd been to weddings, but they were dress-up Sunday school type things. I was pretty sure that sometime soon Dad would put on that great big, sweat-stained hat I saw up on the shelf of their closet, and Mom would pull on those tooled cowboy boots with the white star on the front I saw down on the floor, and we'd all mount up and ride the bridle path to somebody's cool wedding.

As I write this, Nora and I are celebrating our 42nd anniversary. As you read this, our daughter and son-in-law are celebrating their first.

On the way to their wedding, to be held way up a mountain above Gatlinburg, all the horses under our hood were barely moving in an 18-mile parking lot called Sevierville and Pigeon Forge. Ahead, we could see the faux bow of the Titanic plowing through a fake sea imperiled by a phony iceberg. Across, a fiberglass Kong scaled a scale Empire State Building high above stages where Hatfields and McCoys kill each other all over again every night and all kinds of folks pick and grin.

And all along the crawl, there are lots and lots of places to get pancakes and to get married. In front of one was a bright neon sign that read, "Horseback Rides with Weddings."

I knew it all along.

The next day – in front of just a few of us, their dog, and Pastor Buddy – backed by a gas log fireplace, a flat screen above the mantel and a bad bear tapestry on the wall – Hallie and Kyle took their vows. I saw in their faces what I saw in our son's and daughter-in-law's at Grace-St. Luke's a few years ago and what people must have seen in ours at Second Presbyterian all those decades ago. I saw that all they could see at that moment was each other, and the view was fine.

What makes weddings cool has nothing to with Tiffany windows or mountaintops, with hundreds of people in church or a few in a cabin, with sterling silver or plastic kitsch.

It has to do with two people agreeing to share the trail, with all its ups and downs, and to get wherever they're going together. And when you can see that they just might make it.

I'm a Memphian, and it's been one helluva ride.

“I was 11. She was 12.”

Swimming in Memory

Sometimes something you see makes you remember. You can close your eyes and feel the warmth of the sun, the cold of the water. You can see the girl.

Sometimes something you see makes you want to forget.

As published January 25, 2013

The pool's closed.

My first date was Ann Wiggs. I took her to a dance in the cafeteria at White Station at the beginning of the seventh grade. She was tall and all elbows and angles. I was short and dumpy and all nervous. We didn't so much dance as run into each other to music. I was 11. She was 12.

I'm into older women to this day.

We met a month before at the spring-fed pool at Allison's Wells, a fading Southern Belle of a place – sort of resort, part art colony, part retreat from change deep in the Mississippi woods outside of Canton.

The fence around the tennis court was covered in wisteria as were most of the people. The owner had one of my all-time favorite names, Hosford Fontaine. Ann's parents were there to take the water, my mother was there to paint and my father was there to buy everybody a drink, or so it seemed. It was all wraparound verandas and deep balconies, all Southern everything served family style to all white guests by all black staff in crisp black jackets. And it was also all wood so – symbolic of where it was and when it was and what it was – it caught fire and burned down to the chimneys in 1963.

Back in Memphis, Ann asked me to go swimming at the Nineteenth Century Club, the eponymous representative of past glory putting up a still stately front on Union Avenue. It was there that I asked her for that date. The pool has long since been filled in, turned into a parking lot, and the ailing building is facing an uncertain future, whether it lives or dies may well have been determined at public auction even as you read this.

I don't know how Ann is doing, but I'm feeling a bit down.

We need our landmarks because they mark our memories and mark the time before us and the time for those yet to come. We don't need to honor anything that shouldn't be honored, return to anywhere best left behind, bring anything back to life that's been properly buried, but we do need to mark our place here, our unique address on the planet. When one of our old goes, the one that replaces it should still look like us and improve the view. Otherwise, everywhere will look just like everywhere else.

Standing where Allison's Wells once stood, on the grounds of a church retreat and conference center, looking through the trees to where the pool was, the memories are warm and green.

Standing along Union where so many of our grand homes once stood, displaced by the disposable architecture of fast food franchises and soulless cinder block boxes, the memories go cold and greasy like old french fries.

What we leave behind us, what we choose to save and what we choose to throw away, will be what we're remembered by.

I'm a Memphian, and I remember meeting a girl by a pool.

"Where is the Memphis that asked you to not just listen to the music but to write it?"

Committees

Great ideas and the great vision it takes to see them realized are the meat on the rib in Memphis. Safe doesn't change anything. Political expediency is just as fleeting as it sounds. Running for cover is running away. We shouldn't be looking for committees to lead us. We should be looking for courage.

This week, unless there's a great idea, we're canceling the next committee meeting.

As published May 14, 2010

Creativity goes to committee meetings to die.

"In all the towns and all the cities there are no statues to committees." *Unknown, probably someone shot down by a committee.*

"So," he said to the committee, "I'll buy a bunch of jets, fill them with cardboard envelopes, and guarantee overnight delivery … and all I need to get started is, oh, about a zillion dollars." The committee would have absolutely, positively said no to Fred Smith. They would have told

Clarence Saunders that schlepping your own groceries would never work. They would have told Kemmons Wilson where to park his motel idea. They would have told Charlie Vergos that nobody is going to get fired up about ribs from a basement off an alley next to a dumpster. W. C. Handy would have given them the blues, and Sam Phillips would have had them all shook up. If you want to know what a committee would have done to Academy Award-winning Memphians Isaac Hayes and Three 6 Mafia, just think about Pat Boone covering Little Richard and Chuck Berry.

"A camel is a horse designed by a committee." *Unknown, probably someone who sees parts of horses at every meeting.*

A citizen committee was formed to make the case for Memphis as the home of the Rock and Roll Hall of Fame. It went to Cleveland. The city of Elvis lost it to the city of Alan Freed? Please. And if you don't know who Alan Freed is, I don't blame you, and I've further made my point.

"Action committee is more of an oxymoron in Memphis than safe driving." *Me, who, like you, has been to plenty of oxymoronic committee meetings.*

Committees try to be racially diverse, age and gender balanced, politically correct, corporately connected, socially networked, and … to be sure … buzzword literate. And what they come up with is just as safe, nap-inducing boring, and ultimately ineffectual as that sounds.

Of course, great ideas need groups of people to realize them, but those ideas come from individuals, not committees. Effectual committees come after the idea, committed to the idea. Promising rays of hope shine out there. Shelby Farms. The Law School. The Greenline and Wolf River Greenway. College Park, University Place and Soulsville. The bigmouth bass the size of a double-wide about to go on the side of the Pyramid may turn out to be a great catch. We should let Henry Turley's vision allow us to see the Fairgrounds in new ways.

However, if we wait for a committee to come up with our ideas, we deserve what we get.

Where are the leaders that made Memphis the original that it is? Where is the courage that took on naysayers and changed the world from right here? Where is the ingenuity that took on problems and found solutions never contemplated before?

Where is the Memphis that asked you to not just listen to the music but to write it?

I'm a Memphian, and I'm not on the committee.

"You can learn to concentrate,
to overcome, to persevere,
to succeed. But you should
never forget how it all began."

Overton Eagles Soar

Overton Park is on the National Register of Historic Places. National Register. All of it. Perhaps that hasn't registered with our current batch of elected officials. But, then, they just tried to turn a large part of it into the city's largest open cesspool. After all, their predecessors would have run the interstate right through the middle of it. Now, they plan to shutter the golf course that frames the park's trees, and, for many of us, our history.

In golfer's terms, that would be a shank.

This week, join me, and tee off on closing the Overton Park golf course.

As published May 21, 2010

Overton eagles soar.

For 104 years, longer than any other, one golf course has introduced this city to the game, more than any other. Short and certainly sweet, first pars are found on this course, first birdies sing, and first eagles soar. And they come back for a lifetime.

This is more than a golf course. It is one of our city's storied venues, a living, green archive, open to all and as patient as the giant trees that surround it.

My father learned to play golf there, playing his first round with my grandfather. They teed off before there was a clubhouse, just a stone colonnade (still there) behind what is now the ninth tee. I learned to play golf there, playing my first round with Dad. I've watched my own son's eyes light up there when the stars align and the ball actually becomes airborne for the first time. But that's not my story.

Those wonderful stone bridges; you cross the first over a grape vine infested ditch and magically emerge from the Old Forest at the clubhouse. You cross the others grateful that your ball doesn't lie below, or with eyes peeled to spot it and scramble down after it. But that's not my story.

Consider the evocative clubhouse itself, dating from the 20s, with vaulted ceiling, fireplace and stone terrace overlooking the first and ninth holes. Take in the view of the course from Brooks, from the College of Art, from Poplar, serving as a grand lawn as part of the park's original grand plan. But that's not my story.

We couldn't get out on Galloway, so my friend and I drove in to Overton Park. The starter gave us a choice. Go with the two antiques over there (guys about my age now) or with those two college girls. Yeah, we went with the girls, and my buddy bet me five bucks I wouldn't ask either one of them out. After all, I was just a senior in high school and these fascinating women of the world were sophomores in college. I took the bet. When the cute redhead hit her ball into the ditch on seven, I went to help her find it. Since I figured no one would see me get shot down in the ditch, I asked her out. She said yes. A few years later she said yes to another question, and we've been married for 40 years.

That's my story, and like the Overton Park golf course itself, it's about a lot more than golf. It's about our history, our hopes, even our innocence. It's also about progress. You can improve and move on to larger, more challenging stages. You can learn to concentrate, to overcome, to persevere, to succeed. But you should never forget how it all began.

And how good it is when it's good. Not just worth saving, worth savoring.

I'm a Memphian, and I won five bucks and found the love of my life on Overton Park's golf course.

"There is roughly one degree of separation between the history of this nation, Memphis, and Elmwood."

Marking History

At the end of Dudley Street – quite literally the dead end – there's a beautiful old wrought iron sign and an arched stone bridge with enough drama for Vincent Price and enough poetic gravitas for Edgar Allan Poe.

The place on the other side of that bridge was out in the country at its beginning, three miles from town, and families would take carriage rides to picnic there among the newly-planted trees, to stroll the landscaped grounds, to admire the statuary.

Today, this is the most historic ground in Shelby County.

Sacred ground.

As published August 13, 2010

Memphis. Forever and ever.

Turns out Boss Crump and Ben Hooks were closer to each other than you might have thought – about 25 feet.

What do two Tennessee governors and three U.S. Senators share in common with one Memphis madam? Eternity, evidently.

In one place, Overton, Lee and Church aren't parks, McKellar isn't a lake, Snowden, Treadwell and Bolton aren't schools, and Winchester, Goodlet, Buntyn, McLemore, Mendenhall, Goodbar, Rembert, Vinton, Willett and Walker aren't streets. They're residents.

They're all here. And whenever you'd like to visit, trust me, they'll all still be here.

This is Elmwood and, established in 1852, it is Shelby County's oldest active cemetery. There are more than 70,000 stories here, 70,000 lives led, and among them our most famous and infamous. Veterans of every American war rest here, including the Revolutionary War. Former mayor, congressman and political puppeteer E.H. Crump joins 20 other Memphis mayors, and all the governors, senators, generals, privates, scions of society and scallywags beneath the shade of champion trees.

There is roughly one degree of separation between the history of this nation, Memphis, and Elmwood. Patrick Henry isn't here, but his daughter is. Jefferson Davis isn't here, but his son is. Helen Keller isn't here, but her grandfather is. Robert Church Sr., Robert Jr., and his daughter Roberta are here, along with Dr. Joseph Walker, his son, Maceo, and granddaughter, Pat. Together with Dr. Hooks and individually, that's more than a century of African-American groundbreaking on a national scale.

And what stories they all have, many you know, and so many more you don't.

The aforementioned madam, Annie Cook, turned her Gayoso brothel into a hospital during the 1878 yellow fever epidemic and gave her own life nursing the sick. It took the good citizens of Memphis 101 years to put a marker on her grave recognizing her sacrifice.

Wade Bolton, benefactor to both Bolton School and Stonewall Jackson's widow, was a despicable character by all accounts. He died in the middle of Court Square, shot down in a family feud. The terms of his will demanded a true-to-life statue on his grave. His family complied and his scowling countenance stands there today, full-size, with his fingers crossed behind his back, his vest misbuttoned and his shoes untied.

That leaves 69,998 stories to tell, and counting. Visit. Listen. You'll hear them.

This is an outdoor museum, art gallery, sculpture garden, official bird sanctuary and arboretum – and a public park full of our most public figures and private losses. The arched entry bridge and Carpenter-Gothic cottage are one-of-a-kind architectural finds in Memphis. All 80 acres are on the National Register.

A few years ago, another local historical treasure, Perre Magness, authored *Elmwood: In The Shadows of the Elms* and another writer of note contributed the introduction. Famously from the Delta, he felt destined for his family plot. So taken with Elmwood, he changed his mind and now rests here.

His name is Shelby Foote.

I'm a Memphian, and I'll be under that big magnolia over there.

“He’ll light up like a Zippo in the dark when he sees you.”

Cancer and Cheeseburgers

The last time I wrote something about Earnestine & Hazel's cheeseburger, I was on a train on the way to New Orleans. Since then, we've had 9-11, Katrina, Iraq, Afghanistan, a recession, the birth of the Tea Party, the death of civilized discourse, and other tragedies, but this cheeseburger remains a reliable comfort.

I've been reminded of and in need of that lately.

As published October 1, 2010

Comfort food for thought.

A friend of mine has cancer. Saying that for the first time marks a life-changing moment. Saying it more and more marks where we are in our lives.

This friend and I are not particularly close but he's almost as much a part of the landscape of my life as the city I grew up in. Always there. Always good for a story. Always shared and talked about. If he isn't already smiling when you see him, and he probably is, he'll light up like a Zippo in the dark when he sees you. And he is genuinely glad to see you.

As I get older, I realize that one measure of your life – perhaps the one true measure – is how many people are genuinely glad to see you when you walk into a room.

His friends got together recently to help with expenses as he prepares to do battle with the monster. That gathering had to be a couple of things – it had to be a party and it had to be held somewhere that is as much of a Memphis institution for those friends as he is.

It was at Earnestine & Hazel's on South Main.

Half the women in that packed bar have gone out with him at one time or another, and the other half have probably considered it. All the men have laughed at him and with him, and enjoyed the experience. All there were there for him. And for a visit with their own mortality.

I leaned on the bar and watched the grill man work while I thought about the people around me I've known for decades, about things that work, and about my friend.

A truly great cheeseburger — a cheeseburger by which others find their measure — begins with the grill and ends in the bottom of a longneck. Such a cheeseburger isn't possible on a new grill, the proper atmosphere for its presentation not possible in a new place. The grill must be seasoned by thousands upon thousands of patties gone before, by years upon years of eager anticipation from those that ordered.

As you stand there at the long bar and watch the smoke, smell the sear and sizzle, you hear the clash of balls on felt behind you, the laughter rise and fall from the crowd. Or not. Sometimes in this place it's just you. The beer in your hand is always cold, and the place is always dark. The jukebox is magic and the dusty memorabilia here and there is mystical.

Some say the rooms upstairs served as a whorehouse in the glory days of trains. Some say they play the blues up there better than anywhere on odd weekend nights and serve drinks you pour yourself when cops look the other way.

Everybody says the cheeseburgers are great. Everybody wants them to stay that way.

I'm a Memphian, and when Jimmy beats this thing we're going to have another cheeseburger at Earnestine & Hazel's.

"You'll be looking at proof that right can beat might."

Not Through Here

When I told a friend of mine what I was writing about this week, he had a great story. He was in his parents' living room one afternoon in the late 60s listening to his father go on and on about the battle to keep I-40 out of Overton Park ... too late to stop it, silly protestors don't know what they're talking about, who are these people anyway, yadda yadda ... when they turned on the local news.

As the screen came to life, the newscaster was talking about the protest and they cut to a shot in Overton Park. There in the very front, smack dab in the middle of the protestors, holding her "Stay Out Of My Park" sign high, was his mother.

She won.

As published March 4, 2011

National stop sign.

He'd been down there all alone for hours, his flashlight bouncing off the vaulted ceiling and green-tinted walls far beneath the city, following the course of the old Gayoso Bayou now captured in a gigantic storm drain. You think about history down there. And battery life. You see things few have seen. And you see "no signal" on your cell phone. You realize that no one knows where you are. And that includes you.

That's when Jimmy Ogle, as he tells it, found a ladder and climbed back into this century.

Many of you have been kind enough to compliment me on my Memphis knowledge, trivial and otherwise. Jimmy Ogle will forget more about Memphis before he goes to bed tonight than I'll ever know. He generously shares it on his walking tours, and with anyone he thinks might want to know. And I always want to know more of what Jimmy knows.

This week, he emailed me to remind me that this is the week in 1971 when a few extraordinary, dedicated Memphians stopped the federal government cold. This is the 40th anniversary of the Supreme Court's landmark decision in Citizens to Preserve Overton Park v. Volpe, Secretary of Transportation.

Anona Stoner – my in-laws' next-door neighbor and, literally, a little old lady in tennis shoes – stopped an entire interstate. She had the help of folks like Dr. Arlo Smith, William Deupree, Sunshine Snyder (love that name), Sarah Hines and others, and they all had Don Quixote lawyer Charlie Newman tilting for them. Except, this time, against all the wind Washington and many city leaders could blow, they brought this windmill down.

A gargantuan concrete culvert full of traffic didn't replace 30 irreplaceable acres of old forest and run over public interest and Midtown. Many of the best memories of a city and those yet to be weren't lost in the exhaust. Our zoo became world-class, Brooks and the College of Art expanded, the Levitt Shell was saved, and new houses sprang up in the corridor, when all would have been thrown under the trucks.

I-40 did not go through Overton Park.

The feds were so sure they could bully their way through, they destroyed everything in the intended path right up to the east and west edges of the park without ever seriously considering anything else. The Supreme Court determined that the government didn't exercise prudence in judgment nor seek feasible alternatives to the use of public land just because it was cheaper.

They forgot it belonged to us.

Anona, Charlie and the Citizens to Preserve Overton Park reminded them. Jimmy is a member of that group today, and Charlie Newman still practices law.

If you run into Charlie at The Little Tea Shop where he's more of a staple than the cornbread sticks, you might just say thanks. You'll be looking at proof that right can beat might.

I'm a Memphian, and we don't much like big government, federal or state, directing local traffic.

"I believe it's a time to look
inside to places only
you can visit ..."

Ghost of Christmas Past

Merry Christmas, y'all.

As published December 24, 2010

Christmas time.

It was my first time to England, first time overseas, and prime time for The Beatles, The Rolling Stones, Soho and the rocking HQ for the whole British invasion.

It was time to discover pubs, and Scottish eggs, bubble & squeak and spotted dick. Time to discover that bitter, served warm, is twice as strong as our brew, that a British pint holds 20 oz. instead of our 16, and that all of that explains why your knees don't work after three of them.

It was time to learn about language barriers, say, American vs. English. Ask to see some pants, as I did at Harrods, and a prig in a morning suit will show you a table full of underwear. "Oh, you must mean trousers," he sardonically oozed.

It was time to learn about time. Walking by six churches 300 years old to visit one 900 years old. Visiting Shakespeare at Stratford and Henry at Hampton. Standing on stone steps at Oxford with Dad, and putting our feet where so many have gone before that they weren't so much steps anymore but troughs, worn down by their witness to centuries.

It was Christmas time.

It was the last Christmas all three sons would share with our parents, although none of us knew that at the time, and the last Christmas I would be single, and I guarantee neither Nora nor I knew that at the time. Both brothers were living in greater London, Jim in Kensington and Frank in Barnes, a town on the Thames not far from the city.

It was time to come home.

In Barnes, I was introduced to a tiny, ancient pub. It wasn't even on a road, accessible only by footpath between houses. Throwing darts, it was my turn to buy. After working my way to the crowded bar and leaning in to order my pints, I heard someone say, "Danny?" In a small town outside of London, in a pub known only to locals, I found myself standing next to someone I was in the third grade with at Memphis State Training School and hadn't seen since he'd moved away in the middle of that school year.

A lifetime ago, across oceans and centuries, my family and I shared a Christmas I will never forget. Tied to a larger world. Still tied to each other. Still tied to home.

Whatever your faith, whether you believe this is a time of anticipation and arrival, or of reflection or celebration, or of renewal or recognition – or all of those – I believe it's a time to look inside to places only you can visit, to look at the paths traveled and at those who've shared the journey then and now, and to know, truly know, you are not alone. There, at Christmas time, I can find love. And peace. And hope.

I'm a Memphian, and I wish for you and yours all that you wish for yourselves this Christmas and in the coming year.

"You can feel the river,
and hear them in the quiet."

Exploring the Cutoffs

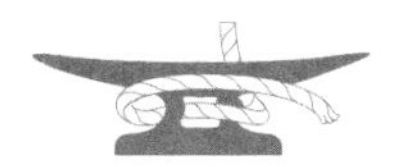

You can go with the flow, sticking to the mainstream, the current if you will, where the most noise and the most traffic are, where most of us test the wind and tack for position.

Or you can travel to where we've been, and quietly discover brand new ways to look at who we are on almost forgotten paths.

As published February 25, 2011

See what you can catch.

When the river determined its own course, before it got its man-made shoulders, before spring disaster and all-year fear made us try to tame it, it went where it wanted and – like the biggest bully in the school-yard, the meanest drunk in the bar – directed its fury against those who talked back.

Think of it as original eminent domain.

When the river decided to change its course, it abandoned its own bends and curves, cutting them off and creating new banks, leaving new islands and lakes in its wake.

As it ceaselessly pushed its progress south, the stiller world left behind brought new experiences from old man river's legacy.

These are quieter, calmer places – even soothing – like a beer at sunset on a Horseshoe dock, the aptly named Arkansas oxbow, or a bass boated in the Tunica Cutoff, a good bet long before there were legal casinos in Mississippi, or skiing around a Moon Lake island, where there once was an illegal casino in Mississippi.

Other cutoffs close at hand are worthy of exploration – modern day, dry land versions formed by the relentless progress of concrete and roadways, of making new plans for tomorrows and leaving our yesterdays behind.

One is just south of the Memphis-Arkansas Bridge, once our bustling gateway, now isolated by ever increasing lanes, ever rising barriers.

Here you can mine the unique assets of the National Ornamental Metal Museum, the mounds of the Chickasaw, and the haunting history of those who would seek to conquer the Mississippi and pay the price.

You can explore two parks, DeSoto and Crump, standing on a fort battery in one, and accessing the catwalk-like bridge walkway from the other, feeling the whole bridge shake as the semis flow by and the river flows beneath.

Here is the pride of Kemmons Wilson's new chain when it was built in the 50s, its glass-walled, fifth floor dining room affording a stunning view of the river. Now a fading Super 8 Motel, scaling its heights to a fifth floor balcony still shows you the view and allows a peek into the mysterious, abandoned Marine Hospital grounds behind it.

You can see the imposing hospital built in 1936, but you can see that from the ground. From here you can see the original hospital, a deep-porched, metal-roofed elegant Victorian lady from 1883, her beauty still evident though sadly neglected.

If it's not haunted, it should be – by Civil War wounded, some say, but that was far earlier, or by yellow fever victims, some say, but that, too, was earlier.

Those who took the air on this porch until 1965, who lost a battle in these rooms, were river people. They fought the Mississippi building the original levees, operating the boats, dredging and dragging land and life from the flotsam and jetsam of a nation, and it broke them.

You can feel the river, and hear them in the quiet.

I'm a Memphian, and I fish the cutoffs.

"Nobody passes a plate,
unless there's food on it."

Feed the Spirit

It might be a great deal for lunch. It might be a great deal more. Either way, you'll walk away full.

As published August 5, 2011

It's good for you.

My cheeseburger was a religious experience.

Melting provolone flows over and through a mound of caramelized onions and sautéed mushrooms, a luscious kind of lava covering a mountain of ground beef, all between two pieces of a toasted artisan bun fighting, and losing, a battle to contain the whole eruption. What happens when flavors this diverse come together – in this sandwich and in this place – can restore your faith.

This cheeseburger was roughly the size of my head but still smaller than the heart of the woman who served it to me – Onie Johns, founder of Caritas Village. It's kind of a campus on Harvard Avenue, a block from Yale Avenue, but as far from Ivy League association as Binghampton is from Cambridge and New Haven. It occupies an abandoned Masonic Lodge in a neighborhood of once-proud churches and once-proud, blue-collar dreams, but what she and her supporters have done is wake up the neighborhood and in so doing, let it dream again.

My bowl of chicken vegetable soup was a revelation.

You might have had soup like this before, the kind where the first bite begs the second and the second begs description and clarification. Kinda like your momma's vegetable soup, but a little spicier, a little more adventurous than that. Kinda like your vegetable soup, but a whole lot better than that, and you want a whole lot more. It's not necessary to understand the mystery of why it tastes so right, just take it in and let it warm you.

My second bowl was an affirmation.

Onie doesn't talk it, she lives it. She moved in down the street a decade ago and opened Caritas Village four years ago. Her son-in-law – trained at the American Culinary Institute – moved into the kitchen. And, trust me, you're going to be moved by what comes out of there.

Gardens from all over the neighborhood supply the produce, and all around you, people from all over the Memphis landscape are together at table. Upstairs, there's a community theatre, an artist-in-residence-program, the Hope Gallery, a passel of kids most of the time and something going on all the time. Nobody preaches, but the sermon is pretty clear. Nobody passes a plate, unless there's food on it. Most of all, nobody wags a self-righteous finger and tells you what you're supposed to do or be like.

It's right in front of you.

This from the homepage, "Caritas Village seeks to break down walls of hostility between and among neighboring cultures, and build bridges of love and trust between the rich and those made poor." This concerning what hangs in the gallery, "work that stimulates dialogue in the community as well as generates new ideas and involvement."

Onie calls Caritas Village just "a coffee shop and cultural center." Yeah, and that's just a hamburger and a bowl of soup.

I'm a Memphian, and we need an extra helping of what she's serving at the corner of Harvard and Merton.

"You can jump in right away in
Memphis, get to the deep
water faster, and find out
if you can swim."

Coming Home

Getting away from what you do for a while, taking in another point of view, enjoying a little recreation to literally recreate, are always good things.

But if you're simply trying to get away from where you live, neither your life nor where you live are going to improve very much when you return.

As published September 9, 2011

Memphis from the beach.

As you read this, I'm probably on the beach, keeping the sand out of my beer and helping my dogs stare at the ocean. It's a big ocean – big enough to help you forget whatever you were so worried about a couple of days ago. Staring at it properly is a big job – big enough that making sure you don't miss the next dolphin breaking the surface or the next crab making a break for it is more important right now than whatever you were doing last week. That's pretty much the way the dogs look at it, too, and we have each other's back. We don't miss a thing.

One can get a little reflective doing this – and a little drunk, too – causing one to get more than a little philosophical.

As much as I need the break from deadlines, meetings and blinking cursors, I don't need a break from my town.

When I come home from Louisville or London, from Paris on the Seine or the one on Kentucky Lake, from Venice or Venice Beach, from the north side of Chicago or the east side of Manhattan or the south of France, I am always glad to be back.

This is the skin I'm in, and what matters most to me is in here with me, met here, loved here, born here, raised here, died here. While we could look better up in here, get in better shape, take better care of ourselves, we are a smile to come home to, a hug as sure as the humidity.

When I graduated well back in the last millennium, I had shots at cub copywriting jobs at Leo Burnett in Chicago, McCann Erickson in New York, a Santa Barbara boutique and an ad agency in Memphis. The money was about the same – 600 whole dollars a month – and I knew I could survive on that in Memphis. We were just married, and Nora had a job that could transfer here. We could also sponge meals and laundry off parents.

We're still here, and while I'll always be curious about what might have happened if I'd pursued those jobs, I'll never be sorry.

You can jump in right away in Memphis, get to the deep water faster, and find out if you can swim. If you really want to address America's urban challenges, there's no better laboratory for discovery. If you really want to raise a family in the real world, there's no warmer, greener ground.

But you have to jump in. You have to look for answers, and hiding from a problem is no answer at all. From behind walls and gates, from way up high on a balcony, Memphis and this beach can be distant, abstract things.

From down here, you can recognize and respect the danger, but you can also feel the breeze and the power, get the place between your toes, and watch for your wave.

I'm a Memphian, and I just saw a whole school of dolphins out there.

“When they go, unfairly young or fairly relieved of pain, a part of us goes as well.”

For Bob

I once met Bob Hope.

He was appearing on my college campus and my roommate and I thought it might be a good idea to make him an honorary member of our frat. Why? Well, we'd heard his son was an ATO at Arizona. And I was the public information officer for the chapter. And we'd had a lot of beer. And ... aw, what the hell ... so we climbed a fire escape and through the window into the hall of a hotel and knocked on his suite door. Amazingly, he came to the door. I gave him my pin and he graciously accepted it and shut the door.

It never occurred to either of us to bring a camera, or that I would never see my pin again, or that absolutely no one would believe us, or that drunk is no way to climb a fire escape.

But Bob and I have that memory. Not Bob Hope, the honorary ATO, but Bob Alley, the roommate.

And right now, Hope's theme song, "Thanks For The Memory," seems all too appropriate.

As published January 13, 2012

Found, not lost.

"There's a hole up here," she said, and then held up a mirror so I could see a perfectly round, barren wasteland about two inches wide in what used to be an uninterrupted forest of dark brown hair. But, then, it used be all dark brown, too. "What should I do about it?" I asked. "Stay away from people taller than you," she said.

Cute, Jean, very cute.

Jean is the woman who cuts my hair, and the first time she did that, she was a teenager and we talked about a brand-new movie. *Rocky*. The first one. As in, "Yo, Adrian." As in 1976.

Last week, she did it again and, like the hundreds of times before, we did what we do. We talked about our lives, our city, our aches and pains. Things funny and not. Things curious and not. Life. But this time the therapy session was deeper, the hole up there more prophetic, the memories evoked tinged with something more palpable.

The memory of a 17-year-old kid from Florida who had never seen snow, and when he did see it way up on a mountain on our ATO pledge retreat, he stole the faculty advisor's car, drove as far up there as he could, and walked the rest of the way to play in it.

The memory of him taking me for a cup of coffee at Dunkin' Donuts in Fort Lauderdale. In his plane. Flying low over Miami Beach just after dawn, and so low over the Everglades you felt you could reach out and touch the waving sea of grass. We laughed a lot.

Last week, I delivered a eulogy for Bob Alley. Fraternity brother, college roommate, best friend.

Maybe you believe that connections like that are never broken, and become permanent residents in a greater eternal consciousness. Or maybe, upon reading that last sentence, you'd say what Bob would, "Oh, please."

But I believe this: we don't lose people like that, we gain from having known them, we grow from the experiences shared, we own the memories, and we know we were and can be special markers in the lives of others, parts of other families, parts, in fact, of other people.

When they go, unfairly young or fairly relieved of pain, a part of us goes as well.

We can take comfort in what remains. In the things you think of – in family and friends still here, in the twinkle in a baby's eye and a new ripple in the gene pool – but also in long-familiar things you might not think about much. Things like the constant flow of rivers and tides, the glory in storms, Pete & Sam's Italian spinach, good jokes and good stories told well, and the same barber for 36 years.

And be thankful for the whole ride.

I didn't lose Bob Alley. I found him 45 years ago. Thank God.

I'm a Memphian, and I just got a haircut and said goodbye to a part of me.

“Corporate-speak still uses fifty-cent words and tired old cliches to mask nickel thoughts and lack of originality.”

The Age of Ize

I fear that we've forgotten how to talk to each other, substituting the phony, forced language of board rooms and meeting rooms for honest and open discourse, accepting the abbreviated, misspelled, misused and often misguided babble of the ether as writing, allowing long worn out metaphors to be as common in sentences as periods.

It's getting so bad it might be funny, but I fear we're losing our sense of humor, too.

And that is no laughing matter.

As published November 4, 2011

The izing of America.

He stood on a board above a pool in 1936 and on a hill above Paul Newman in 1967, and both times, he nailed it.

Strother Martin's dive won the National Springboard Diving Junior Championship and entered the record book, and his immortal line from *Cool Hand Luke* identified our problem then and now and entered the national lexicon.

"What we've got here is … failure to communicate."

Corporate-speak still uses fifty-cent words and tired old clichés to mask nickel thoughts and lack of originality. Just go to a meeting or read what passes for a business letter. But now the Supreme Court has declared the corporation to be a person, and the way that corporations speak is bleeding into and all over the way that real people do. We're inventing and/or employing words in everyday application to sound important and/or sensitive, creating language to mask our inability to use the one we have.

We don't call or contact or get in touch or ask anybody anymore, we reach out. We don't talk, we share. We don't send, we message, and we email, post, tweet, text, link, conference and stream, more concerned about the means than the message.

And we're izing up a storm. For instance, rank has been replaced by prioritize, a perfectly good word of four letters replaced by an invented, self-important, pretentious one formed from ten. If we can monetize something rather than just value it, bank on it. If we can verbalize instead of say, you'll hear it that way. If we can calendarize instead of schedule, plan on it. We even bastardize existing ize, concretizing instead of finalizing, systemizing instead of organizing.

Bottom line, net net, at the end of the day, following the final cliché – we're taking one of the most difficult languages in the world to learn – in one of the few countries if not the only country requiring the teaching of its language at every level from pre-school to college – and making it more difficult still. While we're at it, we're removing much of its warmth and natural charm and transplanting malaprop-laden bromides and cold and unnatural bovine obfuscation.

Corporate bull.

As Strother himself said in *Butch Cassidy and the Sundance Kid*, every time his character spit tobacco juice and successfully cleared his beard, "Bingo."

While it seems that punctuation is thought of as those holes in saltshakers and grammar as the cracker base for s'mores, that's not what I'm talking about. I know I use sentence fragments. A lot. Really.

I'm talking about clear communication, and here's a fine example, posted by my daughter on Facebook right after, obviously, a corporate meeting.

"Today's lesson is idioms. You flush out a toilet or an ear canal. You FLESH out an idea. You hone a skill or a knife. You HOME IN ON a particular item (as in homing pigeon). Things that come down the pipe are probably gross. Things that are coming down the PIKE are upcoming events."

Bingo.

I'm a Memphian, and let's be clear.

“The rest of us would just
see a cloudy day.”

John or Bill

A bit absent-minded, cold, detached, who doesn't pay anyone much mind and doesn't much pay his bills. A bit of a dandy who changes the spelling of his last name and the details of his military record for effect.

And more than a bit disliked by folks in town.

A genius considered by many who consider these things to be the greatest Southern writer, if not the greatest American writer, if not the greatest writer period, of the 20th century.

And the winner of two Pulitzers for fiction. And the Nobel laureate for literature in 1949.

The very same and the very different.

As published in The Daily News, July 20, 2012

A prophet is not without honor, save around here.

If William Faulkner looked out the window on this cloudy day he would see the still and always green magnolia leaves still and always sad still and always there still and always reminding remanding back still and always back in the sunless indolent superheated moment between a dark brooding now the even darker starker truth of then and the oppressive promise hanging in the coming storm of repeating the moment still and always the same.

The rest of us would just see a cloudy day.

A friend recently sent me a link to an excellent *New York Times* essay on Faulkner's *Absalom, Absalom!*, that almost impenetrable, impossibly rich seminal Southern stew of a novel. Then, I saw a local piece on Faulkner's relationship with his own town and, in a larger sense, his own people, his own South. So then I was reminded of my own Faulkner story illustrating that point – Memphians and English majors of a certain age are required to have both an Elvis story and a Faulkner story.

Shortly after Faulkner died, my big brother, Frank, came home for a visit from the Iowa Writers' Workshop. A fan of all things Yoknapatawpha, he decided that he should make a memorial pilgrimage to see Faulkner's house. His little brother tagged along. When we got to Oxford, we stopped for a bite at a meat-and-three on the square. When we walked in, we became the object of one collective, concentrated stare and everything stopped except the ceiling fans. Conversation, coffee pouring, even chewing – spoons and forks suspended. This is where I point out that Frank had a full beard. This was freedom-riding 1963, a particularly inopportune time to show up in Mississippi from somewhere north, even slightly north, with a beard. Since it didn't seem like a good time to ask anybody for directions, a hamburger, or anything else, we left.

As we rode around town searching for some sign, if not an actual sign, of just where Faulkner's house, Rowan Oak, would be – searching for a beacon, if not an actual shining light, marking the spot where Southern literature changed, where the eccentric Nobel laureate wrote the words on a wall, actually on a wall – I thought of our grandmother. A former president of the Tennessee Pen Women, she had what she considered to be an objective, well-reasoned opinion of Faulkner – a trashy, wordy, pretentious blowhard, crazy as an outhouse rat, who should never be forgiven because of what he wrote about "us." Didn't care for the man.

We pulled up next to a parked pickup truck, the driver dozing over the wheel. "Excuse me," I said, "can you tell me where Faulkner's house is?" He looked at me, then at Frank, spit something expertly between the truck and our car, and responded.

"John or Bill?"

There is a difference, but you have to see things differently. There, just there, among the oh-so-ordinary hides the truly extraordinary. Look for it.

I'm a Memphian, and we have plenty to see.

"Real creativity builds new boxes."

Bend and Lift

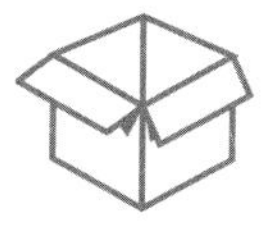

Your first job in a box plant, you learn things.

You learn how to suck smoke a cigarette in a minute or less since stopping to do it is holding up production. You learn that bathrooms are for designated break times since stopping to do it is holding up production.

You learn about boxes. And bigger things.

As published in The Daily News, January 20, 2012

Building new boxes.

"Listen here, college boy. Bend your knees when you pick that up, or you won't make a week."

That sound advice came from Charles, across a huge stack of corrugated boards that would soon hold refrigerators, on my first day at Mead Container. Way over on Manassas, north of Chelsea, way far away from my east Memphis house in miles and mindsets. For me, it was the first day on a job that would last the summer after my freshman year. For

Charles, it was another day on a job he just hoped would last. That day, that summer, I learned a lot.

I learned that a box that will hold a refrigerator is roughly the size of a dorm room when flat, that the edges of a corrugated box will turn hands into hamburger, that my new name was college boy, and that the difference between black and white – between my expectations and those of my fellow laborers – was black and white.

It wasn't that all the laborers on the plant floor, with my lily-white exception, were black, and that the holders of every position above that, with no exceptions, were white. That wasn't subtle. Charles and I loaded flat boxes on conveyors leading to tall finishing machines operated by white folks who were literally above us and literally talked down to us.

It was the equality of the inequality, the steady repression of ambition. Those machine operators, the next step up, made sure we stayed down there where we belonged. We were no threat, because they knew I was going back to college and that Charles was going nowhere.

I had no idea what I'd end up doing, but I knew it wasn't that, and I had been taught that my only limitation would be me. Charles only had one ambition – to drive the forklift. That was the highest hourly wage job on the floor, and he knew his limits.

With that limited knowledge, the people who operate machines win.

"Think outside the box." I truly hate that cliché. Creativity "outside the box" without purpose, direction or measure is intellectual masturbation. Real creativity challenges conceits, alters perception, expands the possible, changes reality. Real creativity solves real problems.

Real creativity builds new boxes.

Some of us are in boxes that have no more room for change, no seat for the different, no greater ambition than to keep what we have – even worse – to go back and get something we think we had. Boxes like this are destined for attics.

So many of us are trapped in the box of not just the unemployed, but the underemployed – the soul-draining existence people endure knowing they're better than that. Boxes like this explode.

We need new boxes big enough to hold and nurture greater dreams than Charles had, big enough that all of us will need to bend our knees together to pick it up.

Small ideas, small minds come in small, closed boxes.

I'm a Memphian, and I know from boxes.

"Having lunch with Roane is like breaking bread with the 20th century."

Turnip Greens, Peanuts, and Personality

Roane has his picture on her restaurant wall, an honor no one campaigns for and is bestowed solely at Suhair's discretion. This is his second appearance, having been there before in a photo of the Memphis Bar from the 40s.

This time, I'm with him in the photo.

Over the years, I've been lucky enough to receive my share of plaques and base metal in recognition of this and that. Making Suhair's wall with Roane at The Little Tea Shop and being called by name at her sister's place, The Peanut Shoppe, rank right up there at the top.

This is recognition of the company I keep.

As published July 15, 2011

Local flavor, aged and seasoned.

My friend is eating pea soup, drinking buttermilk, and telling me a story. He thinks he's told me this story before and he's right. He also thinks he's not very good at telling stories and he's wrong. He's interrupted several times as people wander over to speak to him. A judge here, a legislator there, lawyers everywhere.

Roane Waring, Jr., is 94 years old, as sharp as the aged cheddar on my salad, as refreshingly frank as the pepper sauce on our table and as old-school flavorful as that glass of buttermilk. He'd already been practicing law for decades when today's senior partners were still practicing how to tie their shoes. Having lunch with Roane is like breaking bread with the 20th century.

Roane has personality.

It's only appropriate that we were having lunch Downtown in The Little Tea Shop, a place that's been around as long as Roane and, like Roane, it's been serving up honest, straightforward fare for all that time.

I think it's fair to say that if something was going to happen in Memphis, needed to happen, or needed to never happen again, the people responsible discussed it at one of these tables, even planned it using a corn stick as a pointer and a napkin as a notepad.

Today, a federal judge is settling in over a mess of greens, a former state attorney general is laughing about something with a scion of rib royalty, the head of MLGW is adding to the power buzz, and the state senate majority leader is dealing with his bill down front.

For the last 29 years, Suhair and James have owned The Little Tea Shop, and Suhair might just be our biggest cheerleader. She operates the front counter more like a welcoming center and sports information desk than a cash register, and if she doesn't know you, you'd never know it. True to her beliefs, she produces mouth-watering, down-home-good Southern cooking without using a bit of pork fat. That, my friends, is close to a miracle.

The Little Tea Shop has personality.

Up on Main, a half-block away but still in the family, Suhair's sister and brother-in-law – Amira and Rida – operate a salty-sweet little sliver of local flavor called The Peanut Shoppe. The place is only about two mammoth pecans wide, but there is no wider appeal to what they offer anywhere in town. Try finding Alltree Mix or salted and unsalted filberts in Kroger. They're fresh roasting nuts from everywhere up in here every day, popping popcorn and making caramel corn right in front of you, and don't get me started on the candy selection. Really. We don't have time.

The Peanut Shoppe has personality.

People and places like this don't take up much room, but their footprint is enormous. They have very little economic impact, but their worth is beyond measure. They represent what we have that no other city has – our personality.

I'm a Memphian, and I'll take a pound of Spanish salted.

“Memphians have made a religion out of that menu and can faithfully recite its litany.”

Sam's Slice of Memphis

Sam Bomarito died last Saturday. If there's a front counter where he is right now, he's working it, and if we should some day stand before him to settle up, he'll ask if we enjoyed the experience.

I wrote this column a couple of years ago in recognition of what Pete & Sam's is to so many in this town. Here it is again as a salute.

As published March 23, 2012

For Pete's sake, it's Sam's.

And it always will be.

Turning basic things into things Memphis is part of our storytelling alchemy. Some mixture of food, drink and funky has to be involved in the telling, and the telling should take a while. Sometimes the stage itself may be the story.

For instance, Italian food is basic, but Pete & Sam's is basic to Memphis.

It's early evening in Rome and we're on our way to a little family trattoria we've heard about. We found it tucked away on one of those ten-foot-wide Roman streets that's so old you'd swear you just passed Ben Hur. There were only four tables, and the family made and served everything from the pasta to the wine. A platter of spinach with enough garlic to keep the vampires in Transylvania was served with great flourish, a family specialty. Our son, 17 at the time, took a bite, leaned over to me and whispered, "Dad, this is *not* Italian spinach."

Translation – it was not Pete & Sam's Italian spinach.

Started by Pete Romeo and Sam Bomarito in 1948 and an Italian American embassy on Park since 1960, Pete & Sam's has convinced generations that there's just one way to make Italian spinach.

Pete left after a year, but Sam kept Pete in the name and the menu basically unchanged. Memphians have made a religion out of that menu and can faithfully recite its litany. Catholics, Jews, Protestants, agnostics and atheists worship there every weekend, packing the lobby, and filling the cracked vinyl booths and bad-motel-restaurant chairs like pews. Sam was the head elder, commanding the cash register, holding forth in front of a wall covered by signed glossies of A-list celebs, B-list celebs, and quite a few who-the-hell-is-that celebs.

Pizza with a toasty crust thinner than angel hair, available as a side dish – not just a slice but your very own baby pizza? *Oh, Lord.* The beacon salad with its dressing of one part 1,000-island and three parts Parmesan, covered in diced tomatoes and about a half-pound of crumbled bacon? *Praise be.* The dilemma of choosing between manicotti, cannelloni, scallopini, or one of the best filets you've ever had – with an artichoke and Italian spinach pizza on the side? *Oy vey.* The wine list is great because you bring your own. *Amen.*

Pete & Sam's is not for everybody, but every night it looks like a slice of the whole Memphis pizza. People either swear by it or swear they're never coming back. The décor would have to get better to get bad. Car washes have better wall treatments and lighting.

It's a lot like me – cheap, salty, loud, and, after a little Chianti, in my opinion, a whole lot of fun. It is, in fact, a lot like Memphis – not as pretty as some but not pretentious, full of more than our fair share of good and honest folk, and loaded with local flavor.

I'm a Memphian, and, on behalf of all Memphians, I'd like to say, "Thanks, Sam."

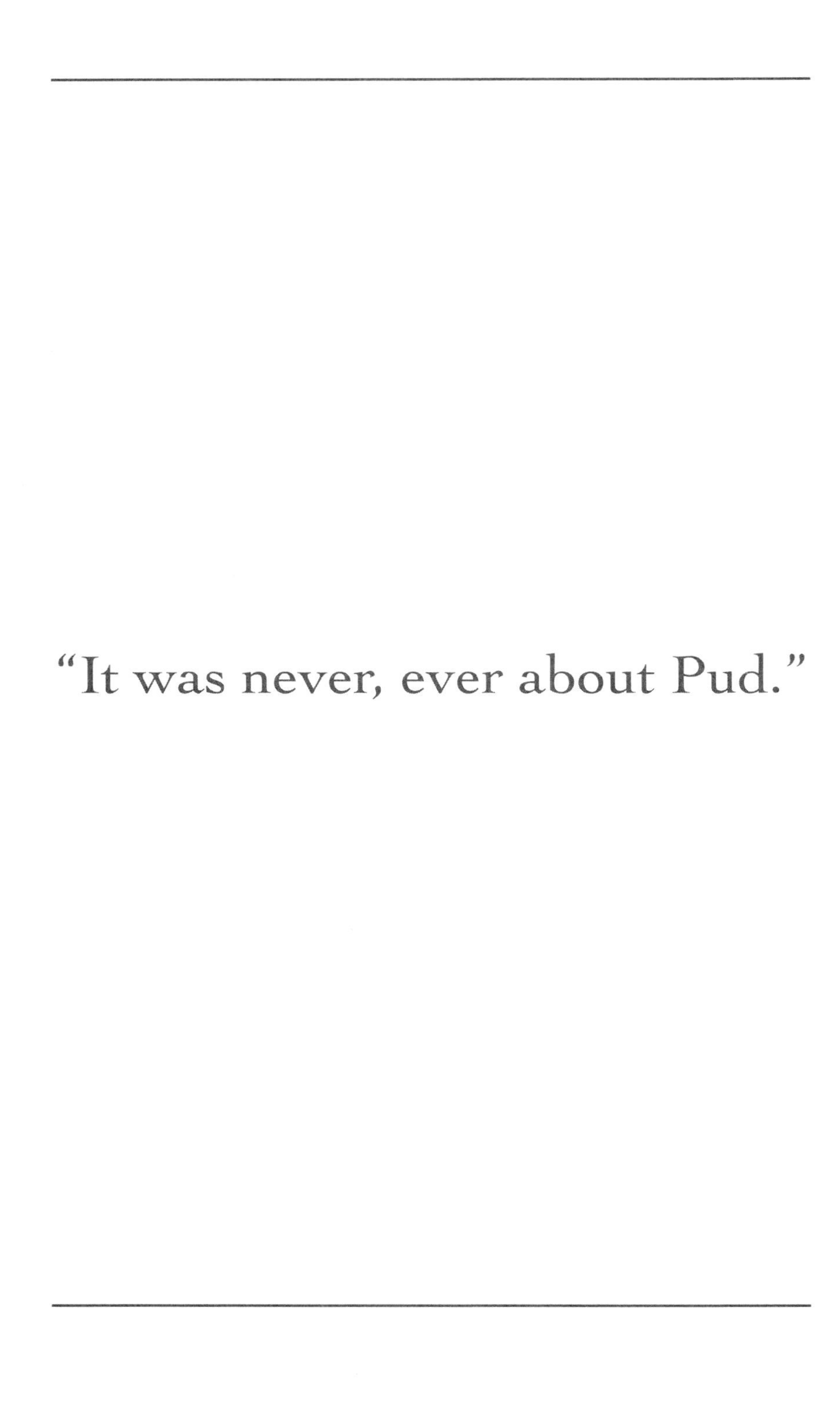
"It was never, ever about Pud."

One Quiet Truck

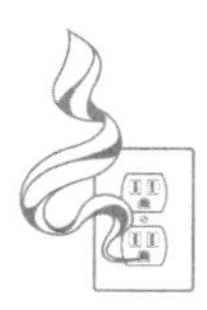

We've all heard the cliché "lead by example," but amid all the self-centered concern these days, the shallow self-promotion and self-gratification, there simply aren't enough examples.

Here are two.

As published August 31, 2012

Just send one quiet truck.

My friend Joan White died a couple of weeks ago. You may not have known that.

In fact, if you aren't a member of advertising's old school fraternity, you may not know that Joan made the boys let the girls in and made the business, and us, better. In fact, if you aren't a member of Temple Israel, you may not know how much she meant there, how her steady devotion gave steady evidence of, in the words of her rabbi, "a life worthy of living that enriched us all." You may not know that she was Miss Holly to Mr. Bingle, trailblazer and mentor to generations of ad agency folks, and just the volunteer to talk to in the Temple Israel shop if you were looking for just the right menorah or kiddush cup. And because of her selfless work and life ethic, business women today will never have to know how tough it was in the 50s for a single Jewish mother from Chicago with a two-year-old in tow to make it here.

Recently, a friend told Joan at lunch that Miss Holly and Mr. Bingle were getting quite a few hits on Google. "Why?" Joan wondered.

It was never, ever about Joan.

As Rabbi Danziger, friends and family talked about Joan, I was reminded of someone else. Someone else who defied stereotypes and pushed boundaries and inspired others by who she was, someone to be like and learn from, someone I loved very much.

My mother-in-law, Pud Ballenger, died in 1998. Most of the people who knew her didn't know that she was the society editor for *The Commercial Appeal* in her twenties, or in charge of communications for her beloved Southwestern years before it was Rhodes, or the author of a book on etiquette, or, in fact, that she wrote at all.

Her father, George Mahan, was one of Memphis' most famous residential architects and when he saw Pud's plans for her house, he threw his away. I once was skeet shooting while Pud watched. I asked if she'd like to, literally, give it a shot. She took the shotgun, smiled, said "pull" eight times and shattered all eight clays. That's when we all found out – husband, daughter, son-in-law – that she'd been on the shooting team in college. When she and Doc, my father-in-law, did indeed break the bank and win all of Bert Parks' money – all of $2,100 – on early TV's national game show "Break The Bank," they were given 78 rpm records of their winning run. Pud tossed them. "No one's interested in that," she later explained. It was never, ever about Pud.

She once called the fire department about a little smoke and a suspicious smell from an outlet.

"I don't want to be a bother," Nora heard her tell them, "Just send one quiet truck."

One quiet truck has come for Joan and Pud. And it left huge tracks.

I'm a Memphian, and I remain inspired by the women in my life.

"He made an eagle putt that was harder to read than James Joyce and had more twists and turns than Dickens."

59 For Danny

If you've ever tried to play golf, you realize that you never really play it, you just continue to try.

There are the rare moments when the planets align and the club and the ball and the swing are one with the universe and it goes exactly where you had in mind and all your problems with the game and with life are in that moment solved.

And the next shot is in the water.

Next week, the people who actually play golf will be in town, people capable of impossible things, playing for the benefit of St. Jude, people capable of impossible things.

How can we possibly miss this?

As published June 1, 2012

What these guys do isn't professional.
It's impossible.

The other day, I played in a golf scramble – a format where four players hit every shot, pick the best, and turn in one score at the end.

And we had two mulligans each (do-overs) and a toss (a throw-yourself-out-of-trouble when you've just hit a shot so nauseating you want to toss). We played well, making putts and clutch shots, using our mulligans and tosses wisely, and turning in a score two or three strokes better than we thought ourselves capable of – 62, ten under par.

Three stokes worse than what Al Geiberger did all by himself in 1977.

We shot our 62 on Windyke's east course from forward tees using metal drivers with heads the size of anvils and irons that look like they were engineered by NASA. Geiberger shot his 59 from the tips – the back of the tee boxes – on Colonial's south course, then the longest course on the PGA Tour. From way back there, with just a little wind in your face, you can't catch a taxi to the green in regulation and caddies are using binoculars to find the pin.

Geiberger birdied eleven holes and eagled another, using a wooden driver and blade irons more unforgiving than Lorena Bobbitt.

A score of 59 is impossible. And that's why he was the first to ever do it in tour competition. And I saw it.

It was a Friday and the whole course was buzzing about Geiberger. I caught up with him on his tenth hole. He made an eagle putt that was harder to read than James Joyce and had more twists and turns than Dickens. He laughed. His playing partner, Dave Stockton, laughed. He birdied the next hole, and the one after that, going eight under in a stretch of seven holes. We were all laughing by then.

After all, it was impossible.

It was the Danny Thomas Memphis Classic then. Next week it's the FedEx St. Jude Classic played at TPC Southwind. Then, saving as many kids as St. Jude saves now was just a dream for Danny Thomas. Then, the kind of breakthroughs that give lost lives back were just a family's desperate hope.

After all, it was impossible.

Who would dream that Chip Beck, David Duval, Paul Goydos

and Stuart Appleby would later post 59, and that St. Jude would today post a cure rate for all childhood cancers of 80 percent? It was 20 percent when the hospital was founded. Who could hope to cure 94 percent of acute lymphoblastic leukemia cases and 95 percent of both retinoblastoma and Hodgkin lymphoma cases?

We should all be laughing.

Next week, the pros will pull it back and let it rip for the kids, and every one of them thinks there's a 58 out there. There is, and if the first one is here, you don't want to miss it.

After all, there's beer, pronto pups, and laughter. And everything's possible.

I'm a Memphian, and this is our stop on the PGA Tour.

“They sold monkeys.”

Shared Bites

We both remembered a very different time, and because we were reminded of things shared instead of things denied, we share the hope of a better city.

As published March 15, 2013

Of Katz and rats, dads and donuts.

Howard and I were having breakfast. It was supposed to be about business. Turns out it was about monkeys and parakeets and donuts and dawns and day-olds, about his Memphis and mine, about ours.

Something one of us said reminded us of Katz Drug Store and we were off, transported to that exotic world beneath the huge turning cat head, a drug store bigger than any other, barely big enough to hold all the little boy fascination crammed into its two stories.

They sold monkeys.

"Oh hell yes I remember Katz," Howard said. "I bought my

school supplies and went to the pet department. I was poking at the monkey through the cage with a little six-inch ruler when he grabbed it, broke it to pieces, and then threw them at me. Stuck his tongue out, too."

They sold parakeets.

Ours was named Samson. I spent hours by his cage in the living room saying one word over and over because I'd heard you could make a parakeet talk. Samson remained mum so I gave up. One day as I was playing in my room, the front door opened and my grandmother and a friend of hers came in. I heard Samson greet them. "Shit," he said, "shit, shit, shit."

"Oh, shit," I said to myself.

Across Lamar from Katz was just about the sweetest place I knew. My father would wake me up sometimes just before sunrise and the two of us would go to Thornton's Donuts, arriving just as they came out of the oven, melting in our mouths as the sun melted the darkness. Dad and me and hot donuts.

Sweet.

Like me, Howard went to Katz, and to Thornton's, too, with his dad. Like me, he'd sometimes go to Thornton's with some buddies after swimming at the public pool. Stretching nickels buying cheaper "cripples," the insensitively named broken donuts, and "day-olds." Marveling at the size of the fat rats out back, big as possums by virtue of living between a donut shop and a huge grain elevator.

But Howard and I were not alike. Even though we were in those same places at the same time, we were not the same. My public pool was in the Fairgrounds; Howard's was in Orange Mound. At Katz, he'd have his water fountain and I'd have mine.

But that funky triangle bounded by Park, Lamar and Airways would be the first shopping center where things would start to change, where black and white Memphis would mix and mingle, where Memphis would start to look like Memphis.

Even these many years later, there are many who would still deny that view, refusing to see that we share each other's destiny, but on this morning two old friends shared common memories in a way that wouldn't have been possible when those memories were made.

I'm a Memphian, and the other day I had breakfast with another one just like me.

"Sharing a trail can give new meaning to sharing views."

Getting Over It

Over there and over here. Out there, in here, and down there. Us, them and those. Ours and theirs.

It's time for a new bridge and a new vantage point.

As published February 18, 2011

Getting over the big divide.

Outside, it was a beautiful spring day. Inside, it was a dark afternoon in engineering science lab. In front of me was a pile of balsa wood, popsicle sticks, string, rubber bands and a slide rule. The assignment – design and build a bridge. At that moment – while I was trying to figure out whether the number on my slide rule was 10,000, 100,000 or ten million, while those around me began to conquer canyons with their popsicle sticks – at that moment I knew I would not be an architect.

Bridges are magic.

They connect, enable, overcome, elevate. They make big things possible when they weren't before. They make it reachable for the many rather than the few, doable, accessible. I can continue on a path, finish a journey.

I can get there from here. And I can get back.

They inspire, too. The bolts in their bones that master the mysterious forces of nature, the breadth of their spans that takes our breath away, the height of their towers and the might of their cables that suggest the work of giants rather than mere mortals. The very fact that they exist is a symbol of human accomplishment, testimony to the human spirit.

Come on. Tell me you don't get a little rise every time you drive across a bridge 20 stories above the most powerful river in America. How strong is that rail? Just how many trucks are on this thing right now?

Imagine walking or biking across. Imagine a view of our skyline like no other, pausing over the churning current for the long view past the Hernando DeSoto Bridge to the north and around the big bend to the south. A soaring city on a bluff over here, the oxbows and wildlife over there, and the reason we're here at all flowing far below.

You can get a taste of the full panoramic meal while driving, but if you were to pause to take it all in, you'd find out exactly how strong that rail is and meet at least one of those trucks.

The Greater Memphis Greenline and supporters on both sides of the Mississippi are giving us reason to pause. They plan to resurrect the northernmost roadway of the Harahan Bridge, built in 1916 and shut down in 1949, and convert it to pedestrian use. Seems we and Crittenden County already own the span. Eventually, and sooner than we would have thought possible before the opening of the Shelby Farms Greenline and all the work along the Wolf, somebody in Collierville can take a bike or a hike on a dedicated trail all the way to Arkansas.

Big water, big bridges, big skylines and big vistas experienced up close and personal can provide new perspective for big problems. Sharing a trail can give new meaning to sharing views.

Providing all of that on a people scale is a trail marker for a big time city.

I'm a Memphian, and this is a big step.